Knit Socks!

Knit Socks!

17 Classic Patterns for Cozy Feet

BETSY LEE McCARTHY

Photography by John Polak

Storey Publishing

The mission of Storey Publishing is to serve our customers by publishing practical information that encourages personal independence in harmony with the environment.

Edited by Gwen Steege and Kathy Brock
Art direction and book design by Mary Winkelman Velgos
Text production by Jennifer Jepson Smith

Photography by © John Polak Photography, except back cover photograph by Kevin Kennefick and author photo by www.smilingwillow.com
Illustrations by Alison Kolesar

Indexed by Nancy D. Wood

Previously published in hardcover in 2004

Storey Publishing
210 MASS MoCA Way
North Adams, MA 01247
www.storey.com

Printed in China by Toppan Leefung Printing Ltd.
10 9 8 7 6 5 4 3 2 1

Library of Congress Cataloging-in-Publication Data

McCarthy, Betsy Lee, 1942–
Knit socks! : 15 cool patterns for toasty feet / Betsy Lee McCarthy.
p. cm.
Includes index.
ISBN 978-1-60342-549-0 (pbk : alk. paper)
1. Knitting—Patterns. 2. Socks. I. Title.
TT825.M383 2004
746.43'20432—dc22

2004001522

Contents

Handmade Is Beautiful!

I'm pleased to present new patterns and material in this revised edition of *Knit Socks!*, a step-by-step book I wrote six years ago to guide knitters gently through the process of knitting top-down socks. I had previously taught hundreds to knit socks at various classes, workshops, and kitchen tables, and the book enabled me to share my experience with thousands more. I'm pleased that Storey Publishing wanted to reissue this expanded edition as well. My heart sings when I hear about people who were helped by the first book, and this revised edition provides an opportunity to reach even more knitters.

My mother helped me to see special beauty in handmade items back when the word "homemade" implied that the item wasn't necessarily of good quality. My passion for knitting and teaching others to knit emerged from this awareness of beauty in the handmade. The more mechanized and computerized our world becomes, the more we yearn to create items of beauty from our own hearts and hands — items like hand-knit socks! Giving yourself time and permission to learn such activities is a wonderful, soul-nourishing gift, as well as a benefit to others who receive the special socks you knit.

I'm hoping this book will encourage you to try knitting socks and to see that with a little guidance, regardless of your skill level, making a sock is not only easy, but also great fun. The patterns range in knitting challenge from easy to intermediate and thus support gradual skill building. If you can comfortably cast-on, knit, purl, slip, increase, and decrease, you should be able to make most of the socks in this book. I've designed the patterns to provide opportunities to try new techniques on a small project and thus expand your knitting repertoire. Colorful Fair Isle stranding, simple no-cable-needle cables, slip stitches, easy lace, and attractive textured designs, as well as fun-to-create stripes in many varieties, all find their way into these pages.

Since the first book came out, I've listened to sock knitters, and in response, I added new material to answer a question frequently asked by knitters who learned to knit socks on circular needles: "How can I knit socks on one or two circular needles if the pattern is written for double points?" The simple answer is that you can knit any sock pattern on any type of needle, and this edition explains how to do that. (See pages 19–22.) Most of the patterns here are written for beginning and ending on the right-hand side of the sock as worn. Needles 1 and 2 (with a few exceptions that are spelled out) hold the instep stitches, and Needles 3 and 4 hold the heel/sole stitches. A few patterns start and end in the middle of the heel/sole to hide color changes.

Additionally, three new patterns, each with several interchangeable stitch patterns that turn those three patterns into eight, are included in this expanded edition. I hope they will provide hours of knitting pleasure and encouragement to knitters who want

to create their own patterns once they see how one basic pattern can be developed into others. I also provide information on the expanding sock yarn fiber options, as well as new sock knitting tips and suggestions for taking your sock knitting to a new level.

More experienced knitters, be assured that this book isn't just for beginners. If you're already a sock knitter, you'll find 17 sock patterns, with size and yarn-weight options, plus tips and techniques for increasing the beauty, durability, and fit of your handmade socks. Most are easy to learn, making them perfect candidates for hours of relaxing, meditative, or social knitting.

Yes, it's an exciting time in the sock knitting universe. While almost nothing seems impossible, I encourage future sock knitters to learn by knitting one sock at a time or to knit a pair simultaneously on separate needles/needle sets (see Tea for Two, page 12). This book is for sock knitters — past, present, and potential. May our spirits be uplifted as we bring joy to ourselves and others by knitting socks together!

What You'll Need for the Journey

All you really must have to knit socks is some pleasing yarn, appropriately sized needles, a pattern, basic knitting skills, and a commitment to the project. That being said, a well-equipped knitting bag will enhance your knitting pleasure and increase the likelihood of your success. While you can always discover more gizmos, the few basic items recommended are highly portable, simple, and fairly inexpensive:

- **Needles in size required** for your project (double point, or one or two circulars)
- **Adequate yarn for the project** (Each pattern gives the required amount.)
- **A working copy of the pattern** (Photocopies allow you to make notes on your pattern without marring your book; make photocopies only from your own book, for your own use.)
- **Needle and stitch gauge** with a built-in ruler and holes for measuring needle size
- **Retractable measuring tape** showing inches and centimeters
- **Tapestry needle (blunt)** and a large-eyed sharp needle
- **Plastic stitch markers** or coilless safety pins
- **Small sewing scissors** or a yarn snipper
- **Crochet hooks in several sizes** (Look for a hook slightly smaller than the project needles, so you won't stretch the stitches when you use it; hook sizes B, D, and F cover the patterns here.)
- **Pencil and small eraser**
- **Self-sticking notepads**
- **Knitting bag** that functions well — and makes you smile!

In addition to these essentials, you may also find the following useful:

- **Knitting needle point protectors** or double-point needle holders (these keep stitches from slipping off the needle when it's not being used)
- **Small hand calculator** (if you're likely to modify pattern sizes)
- **Sock heel and toe reinforcement yarn** or thread

Selecting Your Yarn

Once upon a time, selecting sock yarn was simple. Available fingering-weight yarns were limited to "baby colors" (often acrylic and not good sock choices), a few primary colors, and drab "man colors." Blue Moon Fiber Arts and Koigu had not yet been conceived, and the Yarn Harlot had yet to emerge. What an extreme contrast to what we have before us today in local yarn shops, on Ravelry, and on the Internet — seemingly infinite and ever-growing options.

Colors seduce us, as does the feel of the yarn. Everywhere we look, we see an abundance of spectacular yarn: hand painted, kettle dyed, long color runs in beautiful solids and near solids, self-patterning and/or striping, randomly variegated in addition to endless solids. Wool yarns are long lasting and strong, especially when blended with 10 to 30 percent nylon or mohair and nylon. The softer merino yarns are also durable when spun with a good twist or blended with nylon, silk, bamboo, Tencel, or SeaCell, to name a few of my favorite add-ins. Alpaca blends are an affordable treat, making soft, warm socks that hold their shape and are durable when blended with wool and nylon. (If you choose 100 percent wool or a wool blend without nylon or one of the other fibers listed above, you can reinforce the heels and toes with a special reinforcing yarn to increase durability; see Reinforcing Socks, page 148.) And the combinations get more luxurious and exotic — merino, cashmere, and nylon; merino, nylon, alpaca, and possum; angora, merino, and nylon; angora and nylon; and more recently, buffalo undercoat with wool and nylon.

Wool, the traditional choice, has some real advantages for contemporary sock makers. Wool or wool-blend socks have "memory," which makes them warmer and less likely to stretch out of shape than, for example, socks made of cotton or synthetic yarn without wool. The choice of a superwash yarn over one that requires hand washing is another consideration. When I need to be practical, I choose superwash (which has the added benefit of generally being softer than regular wool).

Options to wool are also available and include wonderful fibers, such as bamboo, cotton, corn, soy, hemp, SeaCell, silk, microfibers, and viscose. For many knitters, these are the yarns of choice, either because of climate and/or skin sensitivity, or just because they love them — how they look, feel, and wear.

Looking at the who, where, and how of yarns is yet another element of choice. Foreign and domestic producers range from large- to small-scale commercial manufacturers to independent dyers, co-ops, and boutique dye artists whose small batches are snapped up online as soon as they are available. Political choices can be made based on how green the yarn production method is, where the yarn is produced, and whether the yarn is organic. In the end, personal preference trumps. Color calls out loudly to most of us, as do the hand of the yarn, the way the yarn feels and knits up, its durability, and its ease of care. We want yarn that is consistent with our values, our expectations, and our pocketbooks.

For socks, I most often choose yarn blended with some tough stuff, such as nylon, bamboo, mohair, silk, or Tencel, to increase the likelihood that my considerable investment of love, time, and money will pay off in socks that last. I spend 20 to 40 hours knitting a pair of fingering-weight socks; in addition I spend considerably more dollars on yarn alone than it would cost for commercially produced socks. I think of my choice as "durable beauty": The socks need to have a long, useful life, as well as being knit from yarn I love for whatever reasons. When I buy special yarn that may be less durable, I try to do it with realistic expectations — about the care that will be required, the appropriate recipient, and how often the socks will be worn. And I remember that knitting with yarn I love is a passion and an indulgence, sort of like salmon fishing or making one's own furniture from beautiful woods.

The vast array of yarn colors, weights, and fibers now available make gathering the yarn one of the most pleasurable aspects of creating the project. With each pattern, I've provided information about the type, brand, color, and yardage of the yarn used in the pictured sock. You may substitute a similar weight if you can achieve the same gauge (number of stitches per inch) as specified in the pattern. Frequently, yarn manufacturers discontinue individual yarn colors or even an entire yarn line. This makes substituting yarns a necessity. Or you may fall in love with a yarn and want to use it as an alternative to what is used in a pattern. The choices waiting in local yarn shops and elsewhere are vast compared to what was available just a few years ago. This is a perfect time to embark upon sock knitting!

Selecting Sock Needles

I currently use mainly two circulars or five double-point needles for my sock knitting. I probably knit more socks on circulars because it feels faster and is easy to carry around without losing a needle. However, I love my old bamboo needles as well as my new, high tech, very pointy stainless steel-tipped, double-point needles. Sitting in my grandmother's antique oak sewing chair, rocking and knitting with these double-point needles, I become one with the long line of sock knitters that stretches across the world and time, and I feel happy.

Needle selection can require more thought than in the past because again we are blessed with so many options. I have several favorites in each type of needle. In circulars, I'm particular about the flexibility of the cord, the smoothness of the join (where the cord and needle connect), and how pointed the tips are, because my favorite kinds of knitting (socks, lace, and Fair Isle) tend to be done on small needles. I don't enjoy knitting with blunt needle tips, and I'm willing to risk occasional puncture wounds when using the sharpest points in very small needle sizes! It's all about what you prefer and what works for you. Just as a person can use the same map to get from one place to another whether driving a car, riding a horse, or walking, the same sock pattern can be knit with different types of needles. Although this book's original patterns specify double-point needles, the new patterns do not. You should feel free to use whatever type needle you want for any of the sock patterns. Needle-specific patterns are not necessary if you understand the steps involved in the sock-knitting process and how the selected needle(s) works to make a sock.

Stitch layout must be understood so instep and heel stitches can be differentiated both in the pattern and on the needles regardless of what needle(s) you are using. Know which stitches are for the instep and which are for the heel/sole. As might be obvious, Needle #1 is where you begin the round of knitting, and Needle #4 is the end of the round. If the round starts and ends on the right-hand side of the sock, as most of my original patterns do, Needles #1 and #2 are the instep-stitch needles, and #3 and #4 are for the heel/sole. However, if the sock rounds start and end in the center heel/sole or the bottom of the sock, as many traditional patterns written for double-pointed needles do, then #1 is for half of the heel/sole stitches, #2 and #3 are for the instep stitches, and #4 is for the other half of the heel stitches. Your pattern will differentiate instep from heel stitches, allowing you to work the pattern on double-point needles, two circulars, or one long circular needle.

No method of knitting a sock is superior to any other in terms of the needle(s) chosen. Expand your options by trying them all, then select the one you like best. Once you've made a few socks, you may also want to experiment with different needle materials. Metal needles can be slippery for new sock knitters, but they also provide the speed that more experienced knitters appreciate when working with certain yarns.

Diving Right In

Despite the wisdom of working gauge swatches, many sock knitters bravely sally forth, knitting a sock with needles they believe likely to produce the right gauge or fit based on their previous experience. Sock rounds happen quickly. If you're not discouraged by ripping out and starting over, then you can use the beginning of an actual sock as your gauge swatch.

For example, while wooden needles provide some resistance or drag, thus lessening the possibility of dropped stitches, that same resistance may interfere when you're working with yarns containing cotton. Bamboo needles are a nice compromise, providing the flexibility and warmth of wooden needles, but offering less drag because of their smooth finish. Practice with various yarn-and-needle combinations to find your own favorites. Your preference will likely be determined by which methods are easiest for you and most enjoyable and/or which tools feel best for a specific project. We have many people to thank for giving us alternatives to traditional double-point needles.

Getting the Right Gauge

Needle size and yarn together determine the gauge of your knitting. Once you have selected a pattern and compatible yarn, knitting a gauge swatch is the best way to determine what needles to use to achieve the desired stitch gauge. Too many stitches to the inch produces a smaller sock; too few, a larger one. One advantage to using circular needles is that you can try on your sock while it's still on the needle(s) before you've gone very far. And if you are using double-point needles, you can slip your stitches onto a circular needle (or a long piece of smooth cotton yarn threaded through a blunt tapestry needle) to see how the beginning of the sock fits. Another way to give it a quick "sniff test" is to see how the beginning sock fits over your hand. In most cases, that is how it will fit your foot! This is not to suggest that swatching is unnecessary; it is just acknowledging that we all like being reassured that we are pointed in the right direction.

With each pattern, I suggest the needle size that is likely to work for a knitter with average tension on the yarn. When you make your swatch, this advice is a good starting point, unless you already know that you usually knit loosely or tightly. Those who knit loosely may want to start with a smaller size needle than is suggested; those who knit tightly may want to start with a larger size. It's not the needle size that's important, but what gauge you, the sock knitter, get from a specific needle and yarn. There's

Tea for Two

Knit both socks in a pair at the same time rather than knitting them sequentially. To do this, you'll need two sets of needles (double-point needles or circulars) in the same size. Knit the cuffs on one sock, followed by the cuffs on the other. Then continue knitting the various parts of the two socks alternately until the pair is completed. Taking this approach, you have the satisfaction of truly finishing when you get to the toes, rather than needing to start all over again. The dreaded SSS (second sock syndrome) overtakes many sock knitters who wait to tackle sock #2 until sock #1 has dimmed in their memories.

Durability and Needle Size

Some experienced knitters may be surprised at the yarn and needle combinations I recommend. I've found that to achieve a long-lasting sock fabric, I generally need a needle three to five sizes smaller than the size recommended by the manufacturer for general knitting (that is, for sweaters, hats, and so on). For example, for a worsted weight yarn that states on the label "4½ stitches = 1" on a US #8 (5mm) needle," I would probably use a US #3 (3.25mm) needle to make a sock with a gauge of 6 stitches = 1". Yarns made specifically for socks often provide both a suggested gauge appropriate for socks and a needle recommendation, for example, 7½ stitches = 1" on US #1–2 (2.25–2.75mm) needles. I want you to be happy for a long time with the socks you knit with such care!

no wrong or right in this. The tension with which we knit is as much a part of us as the size and slant of our handwriting. Gauge may change over time and in response to circumstances that may make you feel rushed or stressed.

Since you're knitting your sock in the round, you should also knit your gauge swatch in the round. Gauge in stockinette stitch worked in the round (which means that you're knitting every round) is often different from the gauge that same knitter achieves in straight knitting (knitting one row, turning, and purling back on the reverse side). Here's a quick two-needle version of knitting in the round.

1. **Cast enough stitches onto a needle** to make a gauge swatch approximately 3"–4" wide. For example, if the suggested gauge is 6 stitches = 1", cast on 18–24 stitches plus 4 extra stitches. (These end stitches are ignored in the measurement as they tend to loosen when knitting this type of swatch in the round.)
2. **Knit the cast-on stitches** onto the empty right-hand needle or needle tip (for circular needles).
3. **Slide all stitches on the right-hand needle/needle tip** to the opposite end of the needle. Then loop the yarn around the back of your hand to create a tube effect as you knit the swatch. Drape the yarn behind your swatch loosely enough so that you will be able to flatten the swatch to measure your gauge.
4. **Repeat Steps 2 and 3** until the piece measures 3"–4" (7.5–10cm).

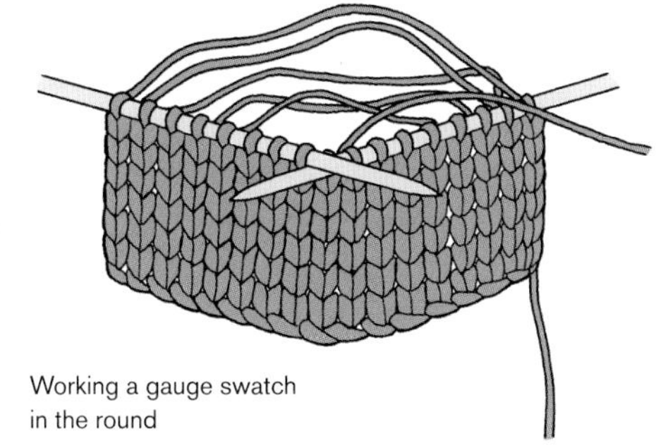

Working a gauge swatch in the round

The Anatomy of a Sock

You can make socks from the top down to the toe, from toe up to the top, up from a hollow knitted foot, and probably other ways as well. All patterns in this book, however, are knit from the top to the toe in the round on double-point or circular needles. Whatever way you knit them, socks are little engineering miracles whose shapes emerge and become recognizable during the knitting process — a special delight for first-time sock knitters!

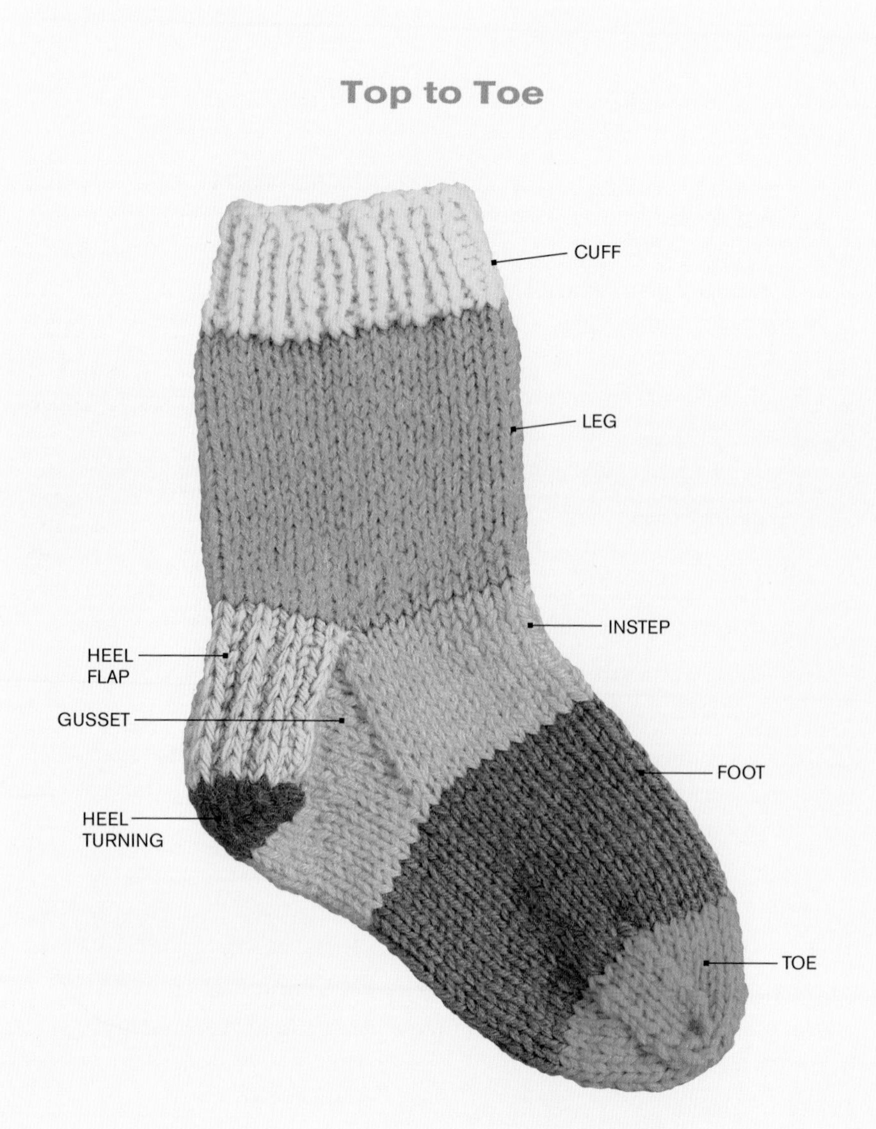

Cuff and leg. You begin each sock in this book by creating the cuff (or other top treatment) and the leg. The cuff needs to be stretchy enough to keep the sock up and wide enough to allow your whole foot to be inserted.

Heel. When you get to the place at the ankle where you begin the heel, you set aside half the stitches, leaving them on their needle(s). You'll use these stitches later to knit the instep (top of the foot), but for now, they wait on their needle(s) while you knit the heel flap.

Heel flap. The heel flap is a rectangle that covers the back of the heel. It's created by knitting back and forth in rows using two needles or needle tips (if you are using circular needles), rather than being knit in the round. Then, working back and forth in short rows that gradually become longer, you turn the heel, creating the cuplike portion of the sock that fits under your heel.

Gusset. Next, you pick up and knit stitches along the right side of the heel flap, work across the instep stitches, and then pick up and knit stitches on the left side of the heel flap. At this point, you are positioned again to knit circularly. To accommodate the shape of the foot, the circumference of the sock is wider here than at the leg and the foot, so you must make a series of decreases at each side to form the gusset. To see why you need this extra space, measure the circumference of the widest part of your foot and then measure on the diagonal from the bottom and back of your heel around to the top of your instep.

Foot and toe. Once you complete the gusset reductions, you'll find it's quick to knit the sock foot and finish the sock by shaping the toe with a series of paired decreases that create a nicely rounded toe. Close the stitches at the end of the toe, usually by grafting them together. Voila! A sock is waiting to have its mate finished and then to be worn.

Casting On and Dividing

Start knitting any top-down sock by loosely casting the total number of stitches onto one needle — one double-point needle, one 24" circular, or one long (32" to 40") circular. Stitches are then most often divided evenly, either among three or four double-point needles (one-third or one-fourth on each needle), two circulars (half on each), or one long circular (half on each tip, a feat accomplished by pulling up a big loop — approximately one-third of the cord — between the two middle stitches). These are general guidelines for three reasons: occasionally a different division of stitches is recommended in a pattern to make it easier to knit; the instep and heel stitches may differ in number; or the total number of stitches doesn't divide evenly on the needle(s) you are using. Details are given with each pattern.

THE LONG-TAIL CAST-ON

The socks in this book are made with a long-tail cast-on, a very useful and nicely stretchy cast-on that should be in every sock knitter's bag of tricks. Other cast-ons may be used, too, as long as they do not form rigid edges, such as cable cast-ons do. The key is to keep the cast-on top stretchy. Here's how it's done:

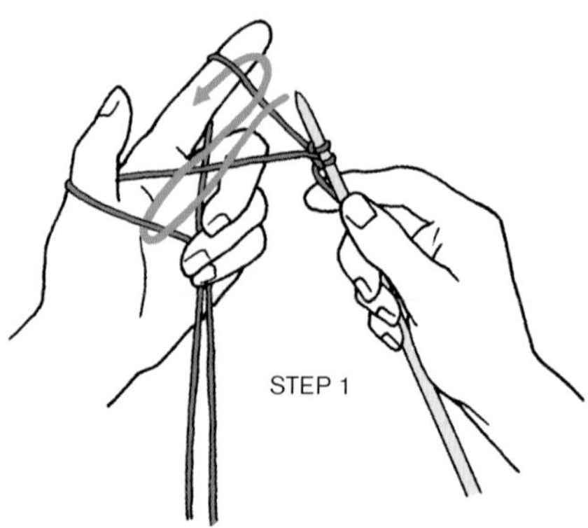

1. **Estimate how long to make the tail** by wrapping the yarn around the needle one time for each cast-on stitch you need, then adding a few extra inches. Make a slipknot right here, and slide the knot over your knitting needle. Hold that needle in your right hand; hold the tail and the working end of the yarn in your left hand, as shown in Step 1. Insert the needle through the front loop of the working yarn loop on your thumb. Wrap the tail from back to front around the needle.

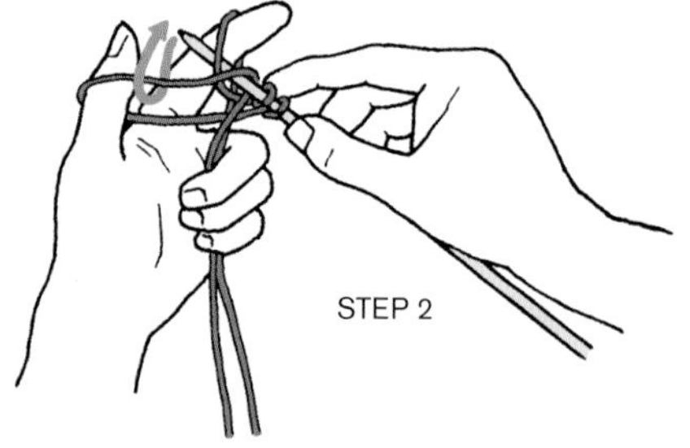

2. **Use the needle to draw the tail** through the loop on your thumb.
3. **Release the loop on your thumb,** place your thumb underneath the working thread, and draw both toward you while holding the working thread and tail firmly in your fingers.

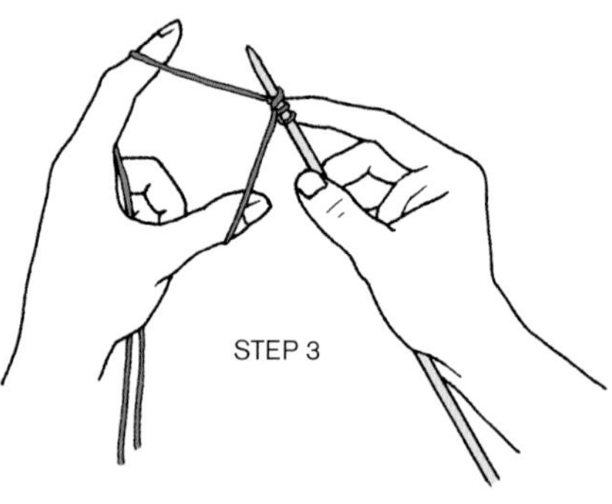

Joining: Trading Places and Getting Ready to Work

After the stitches are divided on the needle(s), the circle needs to be joined one time. Regardless of the type of needle(s) you are using, place the skein so the working yarn will be outside the circle once it is joined. There is a difference in how I trade places of two stitches (the first and the last cast on), depending on the type needle. Methods for double-point and circular needles are described on the following pages.

Stay Loose

Be sure to cast on loosely so that the top is nicely elastic, allowing the foot to fit into the sock, the sock to stay up, and the top edge to fit comfortably around the calf. Practice casting on loosely so that you can do it with the same needle size as used for the rest of the sock. This technique enables you to create uniform stitches along the sock top. If you're still having trouble, here are some tips that will help you stay loose:

- Try holding two needles together and casting the stitches onto both of them. Once the stitches are all cast on, carefully remove one of the needles.
- Cast stitches onto a needle one or two sizes larger than the pattern needles, then slip the cast-on stitches onto the smaller needles before joining and beginning the sock.
- Use a larger needle for the cast-on as above, then after joining, work the first few rows with the slightly larger-sized needles.
- Avoid tightening up your stitches or pulling them too close together. Leaving a little more space between cast-on stitches produces an elastic top band and stitches that can be worked much more easily.

DOUBLE-POINT NEEDLES

With double-point needles, I use the tips of the needles with the first and last cast-on stitches to join stitches. Be careful not to twist the stitches when you join them to knit in the round. If the stitches twist around the needle, you won't get the nice, flat tube you need for a sock, and the flaw will be very apparent after you've knit the first few rows. If this happens, smile, pull out your knitting, cast on again, and charge ahead.

A common way to join for circular knitting on double-point needles is simply to hold the first and last needles closely together and begin to knit clockwise with the empty needle, giving the first few stitches little tugs. But my favorite way is to work a join that connects the stitches into a round by trading the places of the first and last cast-on stitches. I use a variation of this technique for both two circulars and one long circular needle joins.

To join the first and last stitches on three or four double-point needles:

1. **Distribute the stitches** among the needles as indicated in the pattern, checking to be sure they are not twisted. With double-point needles, hold the needle with the first cast-on stitch in your left hand, and the needles with the working yarn and the last cast-on stitch in your right hand. Place the skein so it will be outside the circle once the yarn is joined.

2. **Use the tip of the right needle** to move the first stitch on the left needle to the right needle.
3. **Use the tip of the left needle** to lift the current second stitch on the right needle up and over the first, and slip it on the left needle to become the new first stitch on the left. Pull both ends of the yarn to snug up. (You can also use a crochet hook to pull the last cast-on stitch from the right needle through the first cast-on stitch now on the right needle, lifting it onto the left needle.)

Note: After completing this join, check to be sure you still have the number of stitches originally cast on. You simply made the first and last stitches trade places; no stitches were eliminated.

After joining, knit the stitches from the first needle (held in your left hand) onto the empty needle (held in your right), going right to left (clockwise). As you complete the stitches on each needle, use the newly empty needle to knit the stitches off the next needle. Always work with the right side of the sock to the outside when knitting in the round. (Every five-needle pattern in this book follows one of the needle configurations in the illustration below, but socks knit with four needles may also begin at either the right or the back.)

To keep track of where you are on any type of needle, place a marker between the last two stitches of a round, slipping the marker from one needle to the next when working stitches.

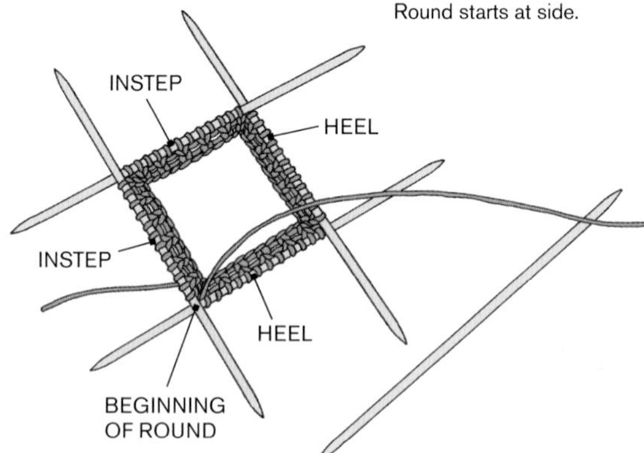

Round starts at side.

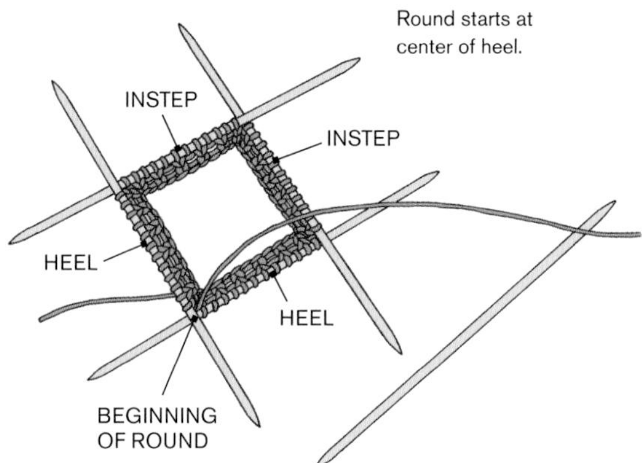

Round starts at center of heel.

TWO CIRCULAR NEEDLES

I recommend using 24" circulars when you knit socks on two circular needles because each one is just long enough to stay out of the way when you're knitting with the other needle.

1. **To join the stitches** now divided onto two circular needles, hold the needles together *vertically* and parallel. Carefully slide the stitches on both needles together toward the needle tips of the open end of the cast-on stitches.
2. **As with double-point needles,** join the first and last cast-on stitches without twisting and using the same crossover, as illustrated at the top of page 18. However, unlike double-point needles, you cannot move the two circular needles held parallel into a tip-to-tip position to cross the stitches over each other because they are connected with the yarn between the two middle stitches. For me, what works best is to choose either of the two dangling needle tips as the tool to help manipulate the stitches. I move the first cast-on stitch from its position as the first stitch on the left needle to become the first on the right.
3. **Use the same dangling end** to move the current second stitch on the right needle (which was originally the first on that needle) over to become the first stitch on the left needle. This transfer can be accomplished most easily by using the left needle to loosen that "live" stitch a little and then lifting it over the first stitch to become the new first stitch on the left needle. Again, when the join has been made, tug the working yarn and the tail to cinch the last transferred stitch up a bit.

The Rule for Two Circular Needles

With stitches ready to work, you're good to go once you understand the one rule about knitting socks on two circular needles. The stitches have been divided between the two needles, to be either instep stitches or heel stitches. The rule is that you always knit the instep stitches only with the instep needle and the heel stitches only with the heel needle. Many find it easier to learn this technique by using two different kinds of needles; for example, one circular with metal needle tips and the other with wood or bamboo. If you see a wooden and a metal tip poised to work together, it's a sure sign that the rule is about to be violated, that is, you're about to work instep stitches with the heel needle, or heel stitches with the instep needle. The predictable result of making this mistake is that all the stitches end up corkscrewed onto one needle and the other needle clatters to the floor. Regardless of experience level, this happens at least once to all knitters who use two circulars, and it's not the end of the world. The knitter need only take a deep, cleansing breath, pick up the fallen needle, carefully back off half of the stitches purlwise onto the suddenly empty needle, and knit on.

One more step must be taken before stitches on the two circulars are ready to be knit in the round: making half the stitches ready to be knit, or "ready to be worked," while the other half are put in a "rest position." To do this, the stitches that will be held in your left hand need to be slid up close onto the working end of that needle so they are ready to be knit using the other end of the same needle. The stitches on the other needle need to be resting on the middle of their cord with the needle tips dangling down on each side.

After all the stitches on one needle have been knit, slide the working needle away from the stitches just worked (either heel or instep stitches) so the stitches are resting totally on the flexible circular cord. You then slide the stitches on the other needle up toward their working needle point to be knit off onto the other end of the same circular needle. If a phone rings or someone comes to the door and you throw the sock-in-progress down, it really is easy to get started again. Don't panic. Look carefully at your work. The next stitch that you should work is the stitch to the left of the last stitch worked, or to the left of the one with the yarn coming out of it. This is true for any sort of needle configuration. Knitting in the round on two circulars proceeds in this manner, working the stitches with one needle, then working the other half of the stitches with the other.

ONE LONG CIRCULAR NEEDLE

To join the two ends of one long circular needle, I prefer to use another tool for two reasons: First, the two working ends of the needle will be held together parallel (and thus cannot be held tip to tip). Second, there are no dangling ends to be used as lifting tools as when working with two circular needles.

1. **Hold the needle** as if it were a squatty capital C, with the two tips pointing toward the right. Hold the needle with the last stitches cast on at the bottom, and a very large loop off to the left (most of the cord). Use a small crochet hook to transfer the first cast-on stitch (now on the top needle) to the bottom needle. (See drawing at top, facing page.)
2. **Next, move the second stitch** on the bottom needle to the top needle, stretching out the loop out a bit. (This is the last cast-on stitch, and contains the working yarn, so it is a live stitch and therefore can be stretched.) Alternatively, you can use a crochet hook to pull this stitch up through the new first stitch and place it on the top needle.
3. **Now that the join is accomplished,** one more step must be taken here to be ready to work in the round. Pull out the bottom needle quite a bit, leaving a large loop (about one-third of the cable) on the knitter's left-hand side. At the same time, create a second large loop (approximately the same size) on the right between the

place where the crossover just occurred and the needle tip. Insert this needle into the first stitch on the left. As you begin working the first half of the stitches, you'll have a very large loop on each side, which led Sarah Hauschka, who developed this Magic Loop technique, to call it "Mickey Mouse Ears," because we all know what they look like! (See drawing below.)

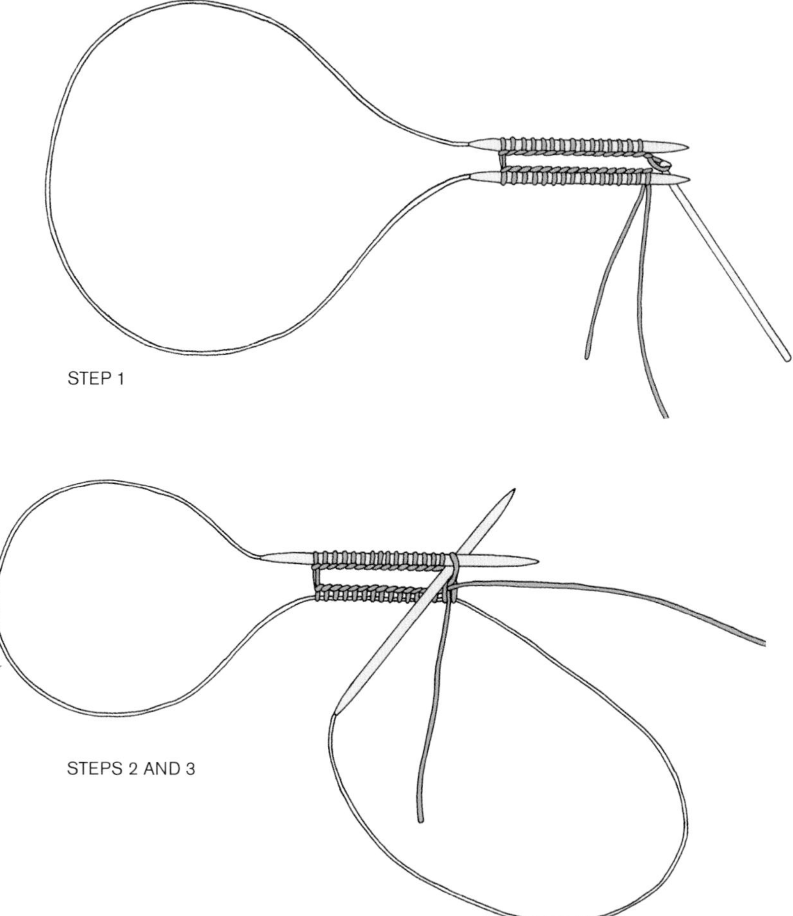

Working in rounds on one long circular needle involves pulling the needle back through the end of the stitches just worked (either the heel or the instep stitches) to create a loop, or ear. Then, knit across the next set of either heel or instep stitches, snuggling the first few stitches up against the stitches just worked, which are now resting. When you have knit all the stitches off the tip of one needle, back the other needle into the next stitches to be worked (your needle tips are again parallel to each other and both point toward your left), turn your work around and, with both needles pointing to your right, pull the needle tip through the stitches just worked to make another loop, or ear, and proceed in the same manner as above. Sarah Hauschka has a "mantra" to remember what to do when knitting on one circular needle:

- **Find home position** after you've turned your work around and both needles point to your right;
- **Find the needle with the yarn attached,** which is the needle tip of the stitches just worked;
- **Pull that needle out far enough** to give yourself enough slack, that is, make the ear;
- **Continue knitting the stitches off the next needle.** Continue this process of pulling the cord to create a loop, working across, backing the left needle into a knit-ready position, turning the work around and leaving a loop between stitches, and pulling the needle just used out for another ear.

On the Decrease

Because the decreases that you work for the heel gusset and toe shaping show in the finished sock, it's important to use the decrease method that makes the finished stitches lean in the correct direction. Decreasing by knitting two stitches together (K2tog) results in a right-leaning stitch, whereas decreasing by knitting slipped stitches together (ssk) results in a left-leaning stitch. The patterns specify which of these two to use. Here's how to do them:

K2TOG

For a finished stitch that slants to the right, simply knit two stitches together by inserting the needle into both loops, just as you would to knit. K2tog (knit 2 together) is generally used at the end of a row or round.

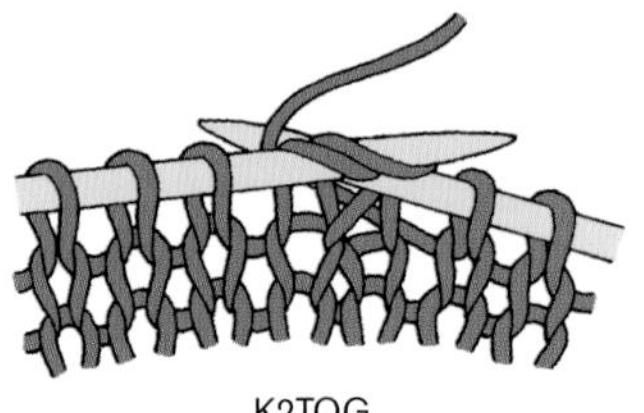

K2TOG

SSK

For the method known as ssk (slip, slip, knit the two slipped stitches together), slip two stitches knitwise, one at a time, from your left needle tip to your right. Then, insert the left needle tip from left to right through the front loops of the slipped stitches, and knit the two stitches together from this position. This technique makes a finished stitch that slants to the left on the finished side and is often used at the beginning of a row or round.

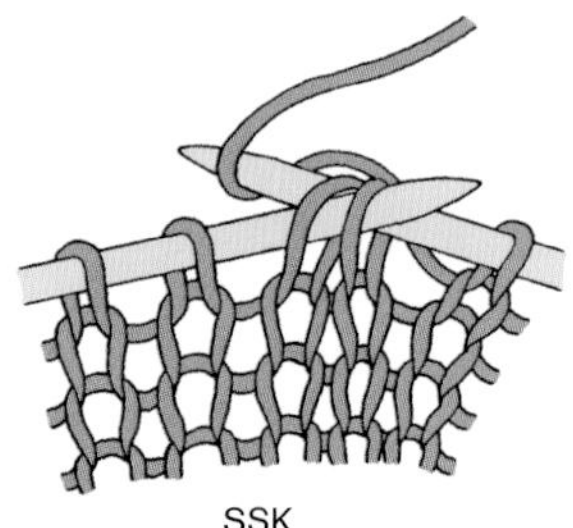

SSK

A Better SSK?

Some sock knitters prefer using an alternative ssk at the gusset and toe for the shaping. Slip the first stitch knitwise, then slip the second stitch purlwise from your left needle to your right, and knit them together.

On the Increase

Occasionally, you'll need to increase the number of stitches you're working on. This might happen when a pattern on the leg requires more stitches than you used for the ribbed cuff. Either the bar increase or the technique known as "make 1" is appropriate for these sock patterns. Note that when you use make 1, it's important to twist the new stitch so that you don't leave a hole at the point of increase.

BAR INCREASE

This is a tight increase that leaves no hole, but it does show as a short, horizontal bar on the right side of the fabric. Make it by knitting into the front of the loop in the usual way, but do not remove the stitch from the needle. Instead, knit into the back of the same stitch, and slip both new stitches onto the right needle.

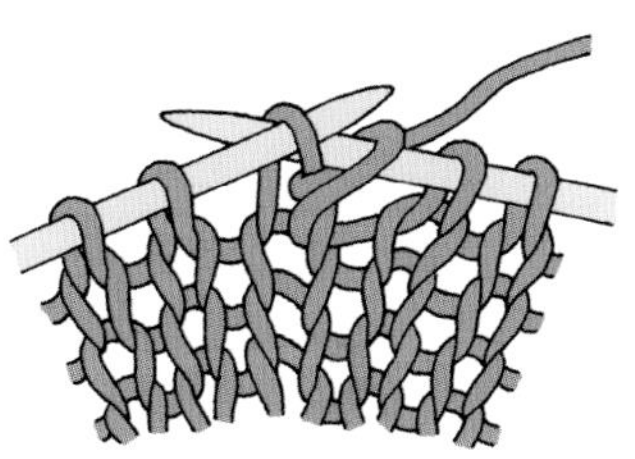

BAR INCREASE

MAKE 1

1. **Look for the horizontal strand** of yarn between the first stitch on your left needle and the last stitch on your right needle. With the tip of your left needle, pick up this strand from back to front.
2. **Knit into the front of the bar,** which twists the new stitch to the left and avoids any holes.

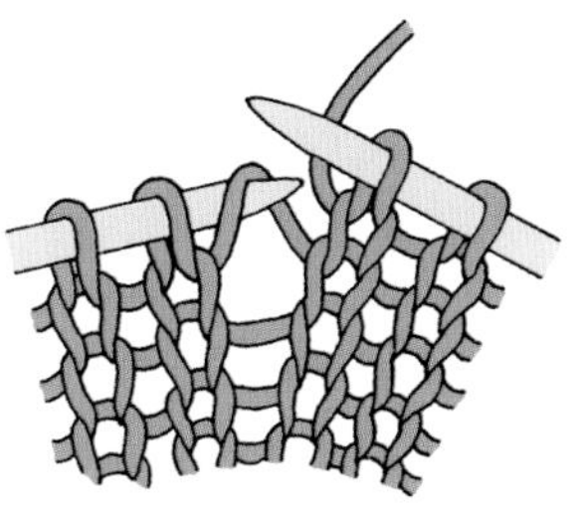

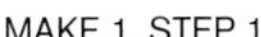

MAKE 1, STEP 1

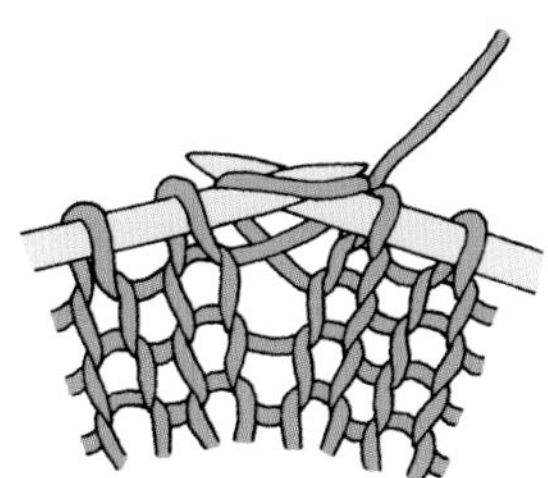

MAKE 1, STEP 2

Adding in New Yarn

When you run out of yarn or need to change yarn colors, try to start the new yarn in a place where it will not be very noticeable, such as in the middle of the sole of the sock or at the beginning of a new round. Here are some ways to add yarn easily:

- **Overlap the new yarn with the old,** then hold the two yarns together while you work three or four stitches before dropping the old yarn. Leave enough of a tail on both ends so that you can weave them in later with a yarn needle. This is not a good method to use if you're working with heavy yarn; it may leave a lumpy place in your sock.

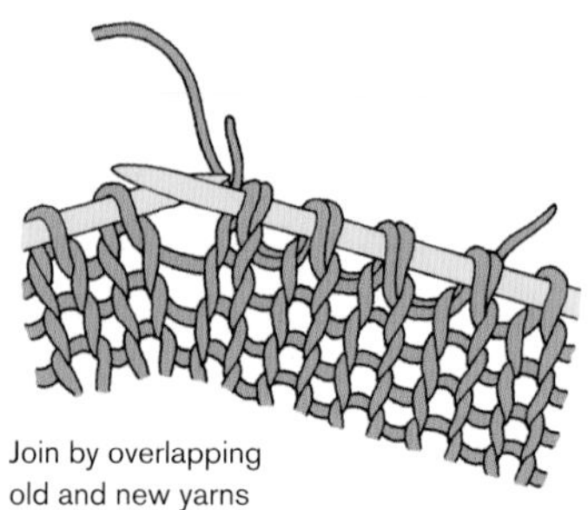

Join by overlapping old and new yarns

- **Drop the old yarn,** leaving a tail adequate for weaving in later, and begin knitting with the new yarn, also leaving a tail for weaving in. This is what I usually do. The first few times you come around to the place where the new yarn was added, you may want to snug up the two yarn tails. And you may even feel a bit anxious; however, it will all stay together — no need to worry. After that, the knitting itself will hold everything together — really! Avoid any little holes when weaving them in by carrying the old yarn on the diagonal up to the left and the new yarn on the diagonal down to the right. To ensure an invisible join, separate the plies of the yarn ends and weave them in separately.
- **When you see that you're about to run out of yarn,** carry the new yarn along the back of the work for six or seven stitches before it is needed for knitting in much the same way as is done for stranded Fair Isle knitting.

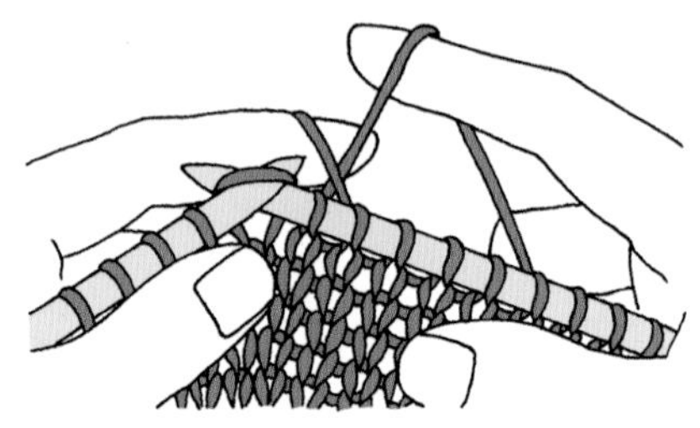

Carrying new yarn along the back

- **"Spit splice" the ends** of the old and new yarn together, if the yarn content allows it to felt. For instructions, see Splicing Ends Together, page 123.
- **If you're working with a new color,** as in striping, you may want to follow the Striping without Jogs instructions, page 58.

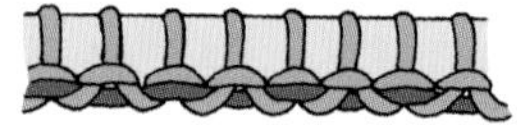

Carried yarn on back

Knitting Leg to Heel (and Beyond)

Once you've joined the stitches and are knitting the leg tube on any type of needle, it should be smooth sailing until it's time to work the heel flap. Remember to snug up a bit after the first two new stitches on any new needle or needle tip to help prevent "ladders," loose places that can show when you move from one needle to the next if you aren't careful.

Many patterns divide the stitches 50-50 between the instep and the heel/sole. Others divide them differently, in order to make the instep pattern stitches symmetrical by adding another stitch or so to the left side of the instep (as you wear the sock) or accounting for a center panel with an uneven number of stitches. So check the pattern to see how many stitches the heel is going to be worked on, and make any transfers that are needed before beginning the heel flap. It's also important to remember that the transfer occurred so that you can reverse it before shaping the toe with 50 percent for the instep and 50 percent for the heel. When moving stitches, remember to slip them purlwise, or "point to point," so that your stitches are not twisted. When using one long circular needle, however, you will pull up the cord to create the new stitch division.

Making the Heel Flap and Turning the Heel

Heel flaps are made in the same way no matter whether you're working with double point or one or two circular needles. The instep stitches are not used during the heel construction process. Those stitches just wait patiently until the heel is formed and it's time to begin again knitting in the round. Heel turning (see You Can Do It!, page 26) is also done in the same manner on two needle points, either from two different double-point needles, from the two ends of one 24" circular, or from the two tips of one long circular. The process is the same no matter what your choice of needles.

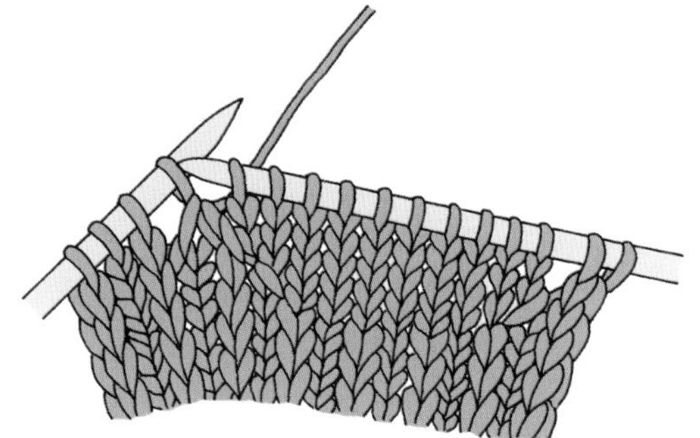

Turning the heel

YOU CAN DO IT!

Someone somewhere started a rumor about heel turning being difficult, if not impossible, to do. Supposedly, this is the part of the sock that's likely to trip up unwary knitters and derail the whole project. This rumor definitely is not true and, in fact, turning the heel of a sock is very possibly the part that you'll find to be the most fun. This is the point when you see an identifiable sock shape emerge and realize that the whole sock will be finished before long — the light at the end of the leg tunnel. The key to turning a heel is to *believe* the pattern and follow it for a few rows before forging off on your own. Like the heel flap, the heel is turned by working back and forth on two needles/needle tips. When you first read the instructions, you may think they can't be right. Knitters are accustomed to working all the stitches on a needle before turning the needle over to work back across it. But when you turn a heel, you work *fewer* than all the stitches on a row, turn, and then work fewer than all the stitches on the next row. This practice is called "short rowing." With each row, however, you work your way closer and closer to the last stitches on either end of the needle.

You create a small gap where you turn the needle over each time. You should have an equal number of stitches on both ends of the needle after the gaps when the same number of rows has been worked on both right and wrong sides. After a few rows, you'll see the gap and know that you knit (or purl, depending on which side you're working on) until there is one stitch before the gap. Then you will knit (or purl) that stitch together with the stitch on the other side of the gap, followed by a K1 (or a P1). This moves you closer to each end of the needle, until finally you will have worked all the stitches. At that point, you'll see a heel, that place where the sock changes from being a cylinder into a recognizable sock shape.

SECRETS FOR TIGHT, SMOOTH GUSSETS

Gussets are those little triangular shapes that provide the extra room we need for getting heels in and out of socks; they differentiate shaped socks from tube socks. To create gussets on each side of the sock, a number of stitches need to be picked up and knit, first along the right side of the heel flap and then, after knitting across the instep stitches, down the left side of the heel flap. The technique for picking up stitches is the same for all needles. Pick up and knit gusset stitches with an empty needle for double-point needles and the appropriate needle tip for circulars. The stitches can be picked up with the needle tip itself or with another helper needle or crochet hook.

A nice, tight join between the heel and the point where gusset stitches are picked up is one characteristic of a well-constructed sock. The number of new stitches picked up along each side of the heel flap is generally the number of rows in the heel flap divided by two, give or take one or two. If you're making a heel flap in which the first stitch in each row is slipped, pick up one stitch for each of the chain selvage stitches

Weaving in Loose Ends

Weave the old yarn on the diagonal forward to where the new yarn is worked, and weave the new yarn on the diagonal back to where the old yarn was worked. Weave them into the back of purl bumps, a few stitches one way, then turn and go back into a few purl bumps in the other direction, and then turn again and tuck them into a few more purl bumps, in a Z-like configuration.

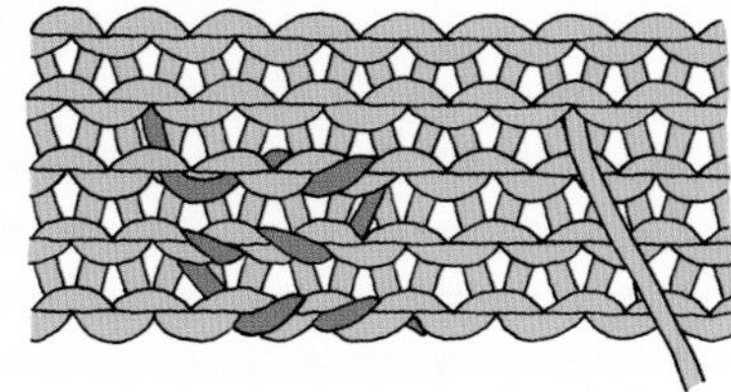

created (one for every two rows worked). You do this by going down into the outside loop of each stitch, under a whole stitch.

It's important that you pick up enough stitches to avoid holes along the edge of the heel flap and top of the gusset triangle. If you're concerned, pick up one or two more stitches than the pattern calls for. It will just take a little longer to work the decrease rounds to get down to the original number of stitches. This will not adversely affect the appearance of your sock, but gussets with gaps or loose spots will. Another way to get a smooth, tight pick-up edge is to knit into the back of the stitches picked up on either side of the heel flap the first time you knit around after the pick-up round. To minimize any looseness at the top of the heel gusset at either side of the instep stitches, lift up onto the instep needle the bar between the heel and instep stitches (on both sides of the instep) and knit them together with the first and last instep stitches.

Tighten up and tack down looseness or holes after the sock is completed. When Lucy Neatby, a well-known sock designer, called this strategy "selectively suturing" in a class I took from her years ago, she made this all okay for me! In fact, for a while it didn't seem like I'd really finished a sock unless it was properly and selectively sutured. Additionally, and even more importantly, it helped me not be discouraged when the socks were not at or above perfection, in every way, once I completed them. Yes, we can cinch up the looseness and tighten things up if need be. It's just fine.

Gusset stitches on two circulars. Using only the heel needle that has the stitches remaining after you've turned the heel, pick up and knit stitches up the right side of the heel flap. Then work across the instep stitches with the instep needle — the first time in a while that these rested stitches have had to work. Now we are ready for a potentially tricky bit: picking up gusset stitches down the left side of heel flap when using two circulars. What must be done seems counter-intuitive or at least highly unlikely. Your working instep needle is so handy and close to the top of the left side of the heel flap, as is the working yarn. However, the rule is that for heel stitches, only the heel needle must be used (see The Rule for Two Circular Needles, page 19). So, reach across the sock and bring the tip of the heel needle resting near the top of the right side of heel flap over and across the sock to the top of the left heel flap.

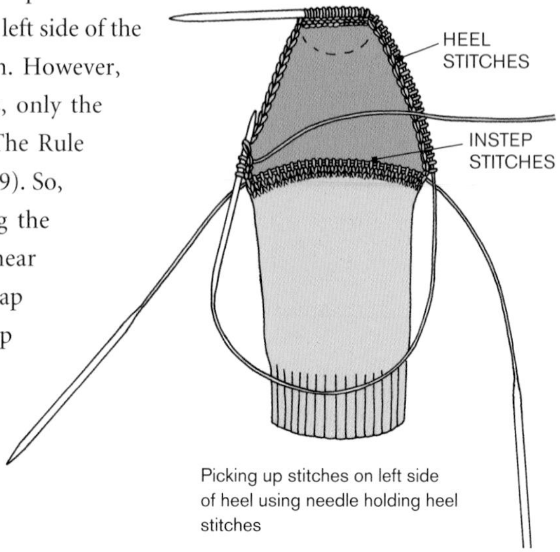

HEEL STITCHES

INSTEP STITCHES

Picking up stitches on left side of heel using needle holding heel stitches

When stitches have been picked up along the left side of the flap, as was done for right side, and the working needle is now next to the stitches leftover from turning the heel, readjust the needles so that you can continue knitting around on the heel needle until you reach the beginning of the instep stitches. Generally, this is the beginning of a round for me. I find starting and ending socks on the right-hand side is easier because it avoids shifting stitches to center the round in the bottom of the heel/sole. There are times when I start and end a round in the center of the heel/sole; for example, when working patterns or stripes, or when it would be best to have any evidence of the beginning and ending hidden on the bottom of the foot for aesthetic reasons.

Gusset stitches on one long circular. Picking up and knitting gusset stitches on one long circular needle differs from two circular needles because one needle handles both instep and heel stitches. The needle tips alternate between working only heel stitches and then working only instep stitches. The tip of the needle that has just finished turning the heel continues to work to pick stitches up along the right side of the flap. That same tip will be used to continue working across the instep stitches. At this point, the needle tips point to the left, looking like a backward C. The nonworking needle tip can be used as a helper to pick up stitches on either side of the heel flap. Picking up stitches also can be done with one needle tip alone or with help from a crochet hook or double-point needle. Back the needle tip into the instep stitches to be ready to be worked and pull the tip of the needle with the stitches just worked out to creating a loop or ear on both sides of the instep (again, each ear is made up of about one-third of the cord).

To pick up stitches down the left side of the heel flap, gently pull the needle tip away from the instep stitches and the other tip away from the heel stitches, once again creating loops on both sides of the work. Position one loop between the instep stitches and left side of the heel flap with the needle tip coming out from the heel-turning stitches. Pick up stitches along the left heel flap in same manner as done on right, using the nonworking needle tip as a helper if desired. When all gusset stitches are picked up down the left side of the heel flap, back the nonworking needle tip into the heel stitches. With loops at each side of the instep, work around to the end of the heel stitches. Back the emptied tip into the instep stitches, in readiness for working the first round of gusset decreases, with the needle tip with the yarn attached pulled out and a loop at each side of the instep stitches.

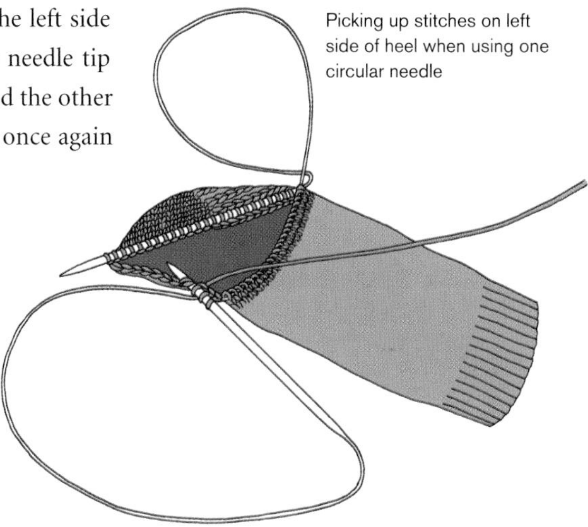
Picking up stitches on left side of heel when using one circular needle

Closing the Toe with Kitchener Stitch

Most of the toes in the patterns in this book are closed using an invisible weaving technique known as Kitchener stitch. To anchor the stitches before weaving:

- **Distribute the remaining toe stitches** evenly between two needles/needle tips. Hold the tips together so that the stitches align, with wrong sides of the sock facing. Thread the yarn through a yarn needle, and insert the needle through the first stitch on front needle as if to purl. Draw the yarn through the stitch, leaving the stitch on the needle. (The yarn in the tapestry needle needs to stay under the knitting needles when moving from front to back.)
- **Insert the yarn needle** through the first stitch on the back needle as if to knit. Draw the yarn through the stitch, leaving the stitch on the needle. Now that you're ready, here is how to begin weaving:

1. **Insert the yarn needle** through the first stitch on front needle as if to knit. Drawing the yarn through the stitch, slip the stitch off the needle.

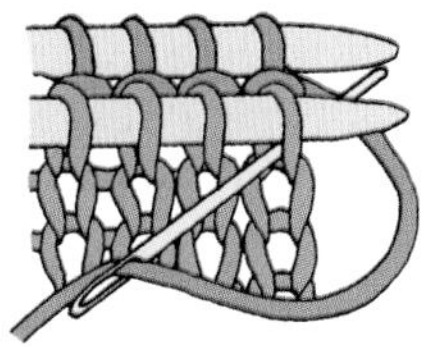
STEP 1

2. **Insert the yarn needle** through the second stitch on the front needle as if to purl; draw the yarn through, but leave the stitch on the needle. Snug up yarn.
3. **Insert the yarn needle** through the first stitch on the back needle as if to purl; draw the yarn through and slip the stitch off.
4. **Insert the yarn needle** through second stitch on back needle as if to knit; draw the yarn through, but leave the stitch on the needle. Snug up yarn.

Repeat Steps 1–4 until you have worked all stitches and none remain on needles.

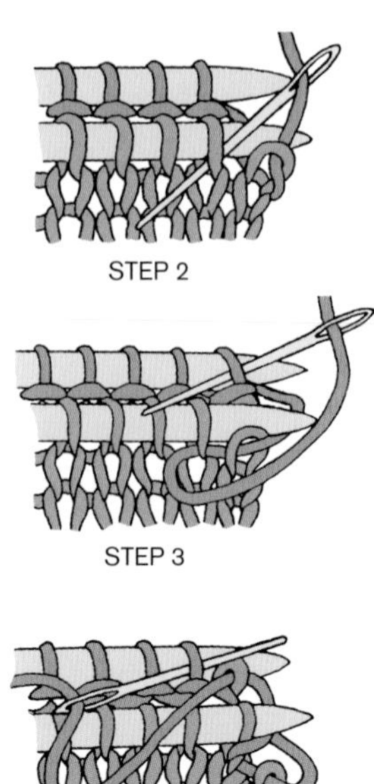

STEP 2

STEP 3

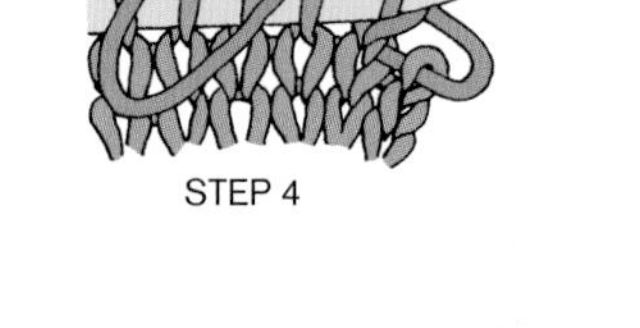

STEP 4

For an alternate closure method, you can draw the remaining stitches together by running a thread through them and pulling tightly to close. On the other hand, if you prefer to close the toe with Kitchener stitch but want a more rounded toe, see the sidebar on page 75.

With all needle configurations, toes are grafted together with stitches evenly divided on two needles (or needle tips) held parallel to each other and grafted together using a tapestry needle and 8" to 10" length of the sock yarn. Now that the sock is complete, if there was no slack accidentally created when changing from one needle to another, no one should be able to tell what type of needles you used. For a top-down sock, the same steps are followed in the same order regardless of the needles used. It's time for you to admire your new sock!

To the Task

My father told me many years ago that if a person could read, there was little that person couldn't do. I believed him then and attempted many things I might not have otherwise thought I could do. So, gather your determination, courage, knitting needles, and some yarn, and let's move forward together and knit some basic socks. In doing so, you become part of a wonderful tradition spanning cultures around the globe across many centuries. Enjoy!

Multiple Possibilities: Pattern Substitution

It won't be long before you're ready to branch out and modify designs or create your own patterns. For example, if you wanted to make a baby-sized version of Shimmy Rib, you could refer to the 36-stitch sock in Peaks 'n' Valleys and insert the Shimmy Rib pattern into it. Shimmy Rib has a 6-stitch pattern repeat; Peaks 'n' Valleys a 9-stitch. This substitution works because both are even multiples of 36 (6×6 and 4×9 both equal 36). Or if you wanted to make a 64-stitch sock in fingering-weight yarn with an 8-stitch repeat pattern, you could use the pattern Off the Cuff, substitute your choice of ribbing or top treatment instead of the cuff, and substitute your chosen 8-stitch pattern for the stockinette. Additionally, to balance the pattern on the instep (that is, to make the instep symmetrical), you may need to transfer a stitch or two from the instep or heel stitches and then move them back to their original needle either after finishing the gusset decreases or just before closing the toe.

Be sure to knit a gauge swatch before making substitutions (see Getting the Right Gauge, page 12). A sock knit in a very open, lacy stitch pattern will likely be much larger in circumference than one knit in stockinette. A cabled pattern may be tighter than one in stockinette because cables pull it in. You may thus need fewer stitches for the lace sock and more for the cable.

Pattern	Total Stitches	Heel Stitches	Gauge (Stitches per inch)	Pattern and/or Multiples
Starter Stockinette, p. 32	48, 56	24, 28	6 sts	Stockinette
Checkered Textures, p. 38	50, 70	25, 35	6, 9 sts	10 st
Classy Slip-Up, p. 46	56, 68	33, 29	7, 8	4 st
Winter Garden, p. 54	64	31	7½ sts	8 st motif
Little Guys, p. 64	32, 40	16, 20	6, 8 sts	4 (rib)
Low-Roll Sporty, p. 70	48, 56	24, 28	6 sts	Stockinette
Yoga Moves, p. 76	56	28	6 st	4 st motif
Best Foot Forward, p. 86	56, 70	27, 34	6, 9 sts	7
Rhythm, p. 96	72	36	8 sts	6
Double Time, p. 96	72	36	8 sts	6
Shimmy Rib, p. 96	72	36	8 sts	6
Off the Cuff, p. 104	64, 72	32, 36	8 sts	Stockinette
Clouds, p. 110	60	30	8½ sts	6
Dreams, p. 110	60	29	9 sts	6
Patchwork, p. 110	60	30	8½ sts	10
Fireside Stripes, p. 124	36, 40	18, 20	4½ sts	Stockinette
Cable and Garter Rib, p. 130	72	35	7 sts	9
Diamond Cable Rib, p. 130	74	34	7 sts	9 sts + 2
Straight-Laced, p. 140	40, 60	20, 30	5½, 8½ sts	5
Peaks 'n' Valleys, p. 150	36, 72	18, 36	7½ sts	9
Simple Ribs, p. 156	40, 48	20, 24	6 sts	4 (rib)
Shadow Box, p. 162	42, 48	22, 22	4½, 6 sts	6

Starter Stockinette

Make these basic socks in one color or spice them up with contrasting heels and toes. Since this classic worsted-weight pattern knits up quickly and can be used as a sock design template, it will soon become an old favorite.

Sizes	Woman's small–medium Woman's large/Man's medium
Yarn	Cascade 220 Quatro, 100% wool, worsted weight, 3.5 oz (100g)/ 220 yd (202m) skeins 2 skeins mc Tahiti/#9438 1 skein cc Malta/#9437 Note: Approximately 275 yds (252m) are needed for one pair in a single color. Approximately 25 yds (23m) are needed for a pair of contrasting color heels and toes.
Needles	US #3 (3.25mm), *or size you need to obtain correct gauge:* set of 5 double-point needles, one 32"–40" circular needle, *OR* two 24" circular needles
Gauge	24 sts = 4" (10cm) worked on US #3 (3.25mm) needles in stockinette stitch
Other supplies	Tape measure, yarn needle, needle and stitch gauge
Abbreviations	**cc** = contrasting color; **K** = knit; **K2tog** = knit 2 stitches together; **mc** = main color; **P** = purl; **P2tog** = purl 2 stitches together; **rs** = right side; **rnd(s)** = round(s); **ssk** = slip, slip, knit the 2 slipped stitches together; **st(s)** = stitch(es); **ws** = wrong side

GETTING STARTED	WOMAN'S S–M	WOMAN'S L/ MAN'S M
Note: In this pattern, the beginning and end of a round is on the right-hand side of sock top when worn.		
Setup: With mc, loosely cast on	48 sts	56 sts
Divide stitches evenly among 4 needles. Join into a round, being careful not to twist stitches. (For instructions, see Joining: Trading Places and Getting Ready to Work, page 16.) On each needle you now have	12 sts	14 sts
WORKING THE RIBBING		
With mc, work in K1, P1 ribbing for	12 rnds (about 2"/5cm)	15 rnds (about 2½"/6cm)
KNITTING THE SOCK LEG		
Note: You may adjust the leg length by working more or fewer rows, as desired.		
Work leg in stockinette stitch until measurement from cast-on edge is	7½" (19cm)	8" (20cm)
Turn work.		
MAKING THE HEEL FLAP		
Note: The heel flap is worked back and forth on 2 needles. The remaining stitches (instep stitches) are not used again until Picking Up for Heel Gusset (page 36). Slip all slipped stitches purlwise with yarn in front on ws and with yarn in back on rs.		
For the heel flap, work on	24 sts	28 sts
For contrasting heel only: Break off mc, leaving 6" (15cm) tail to weave in. Change to cc.		
Row 1 (ws): Slip 1 purlwise with yarn in front, purl to end of row. Turn over to right side.		
Row 2 (rs): *Slip 1 purlwise with yarn in back, K1; repeat from * to end of row.		
Work Rows 1 and 2	12 more times	14 more times

	WOMAN'S S–M	WOMAN'S L/ MAN'S M
End heel flap by working a right-side row. Heel flap will be approximately	2½" (6cm)	2¾" (7cm)
TURNING THE HEEL		
Row 1 (ws): Slip 1, ____, P2tog, P1 turn, leaving ____ unworked.	P12 8 sts	P14 10 sts
Row 2 (rs): Slip 1, K3, ssk, K1, turn back to ws. You now have ____ unworked.	8 sts	10 sts
Row 3: Slip 1, P4, P2tog, P1, turn. You now have ____ unworked.	6 sts	8 sts
Row 4: Slip 1, K5, ssk, K1, turn. You now have ____ unworked.	6 sts	8 sts
Row 5: Slip 1, P6, P2tog, P1, turn. You now have ____ unworked.	4 sts	6 sts
Row 6: Slip 1, K7, ssk, K1, turn. You now have ____ unworked.	4 sts	6 sts
Row 7: Slip 1, P8, P2tog, P1, turn. You now have ____ unworked.	2 sts	4 sts
Row 8: Slip 1, K9, ssk, K1, turn. You now have ____ unworked.	2 sts	4 sts
Row 9: Slip 1, P10, P2tog, P1, turn. You now have ____ unworked.	0 sts	2 sts
Row 10: Slip 1, K11, ssk, K1, turn. You now have ____ unworked.	0 sts	2 sts
Woman's S–M only: Heel turning complete. You now have	14 sts	
Woman's L/Man's M only: **Row 11:** Slip 1, P12, P2tog, P1, turn. You now have ____ unworked.		0 sts
Row 12: Slip 1, K13, ssk, K1. Heel turning complete for *Woman's L/Man's M.* You now have		16 sts
For contrasting heel only: Break off cc, leaving a 6" (15cm) tail for weaving in.		

PICKING UP STITCHES FOR HEEL GUSSET	WOMAN'S S–M	WOMAN'S L/ MAN'S M
Note: If you are using 2 circular needles, remember to use the heel needle to pick up stitches along both sides of the heel flap (see Secrets for Tight, Smooth Gussets, pages 26–29).		
Setup:		
With mc and empty needle, pick up and knit ___ along right side of heel flap.	15 sts	17 sts
Needle 1: Knit	12 sts	14 sts
Needle 2: Knit	12 sts	14 sts
Needle 3: With empty needle, pick up and knit ___ along left side of heel flap.	15 sts	17 sts
Also with Needle 3, knit half of stitches remaining after heel turning:	7 sts	8 sts
Needle 4: Knit the remaining heel stitches, plus the stitches picked up along the right side of heel flap.		
You now have		
Needles 1 and 2 (instep needles):	12 sts	14 sts
Needles 3 and 4 (heel needles):	22 sts	25 sts
Total on all 4 needles:	68 sts	78 sts
WORKING GUSSET DECREASES		
Round 1		
Needles 1 and 2: Knit to the end of each needle.		
Needle 3: K1, ssk, K to the end of the needle. You now have	21 sts	24 sts
Needle 4: Knit to last 3 sts, K2tog, K1. You now have	21 sts	24 sts
Total on all 4 needles:	66 sts	76 sts
Round 2: Knit to end of each needle.		
Round 3		
Needles 1 and 2: Knit to end of each needle.		
Needle 3: K1, ssk, K to end of needle. You now have	20 sts	23 sts
Needle 4: Knit to last 3 sts, K2tog, K1. You now have	20 sts	23 sts
Total on all 4 needles:	64 sts	74 sts
Repeat Rounds 2 and 3 until each of the four needles has	12 sts	14 sts
Total on all 4 needles:	48 sts	56 sts

WORKING THE SOCK FOOT	WOMAN'S S–M	WOMAN'S L/ MAN'S M
Work in stockinette stitch (knit all stitches), until sock foot measures ____ from back of heel, or desired length. Toe shaping and closure will add 1¾" (4.5cm). *For contrasting toes only:* Break off mc, leaving a 6" (15 cm) tail. Change to cc.	7¾" (19.5cm)	8¼" (21cm)
SHAPING THE TOE		
Round 1 Needle 1: K1, ssk, knit to end of needle. Needle 2: Knit to last 3 sts, K2tog, K1. Needle 3: K1, ssk, K to end of needle. Needle 4: Knit to last 3 sts, K2tog, K1. Total on all 4 needles:	44 sts	52 sts
Round 2: Knit all stitches.		
Continue working Rounds 1 and 2 until 3 stitches remain on each needle. Total on all 4 needles: **Note:** If you are using circular needles, you will have 6 instep stitches and 6 heel/sole stitches ready to be grafted together.	12 sts	12 sts
CLOSING THE TOE AND FINISHING THE SOCK		
Setup: Slip the 3 stitches of Needle 2 onto Needle 1. Then slip the 3 stitches of Needle 4 onto Needle 3. Break yarn, leaving a 10" (25cm) tail for closing toe.		
Graft front and back stitches together using the Kitchener stitch. (For instructions, see pages 29–30.) Weave in ends after grafting toe. Weave in any other loose ends (see page 27). To block, lightly mist or steam sock and pat into shape.		

A Slippery Slope

I always carry small pieces of wax paper and very fine sandpaper in my knitting bag. A little rubdown with wax paper helps stitches slide better on wooden needles (and even bamboo). If any rough spots appear, I sand them lightly and then polish the spots with wax paper.

Checkered Textures

Mix multicolored and solid yarns to create a fascinating array of colors and textures on these socks. The easy-to-learn colorwork pattern makes it simple to create your own combo. And the stretchy stitch pattern ensures a comfortable, well-fitting sock that will hug your feet when you're out and about.

Size	Woman's small–medium
Yarn	**Fingering-Weight Version (shown at right)** Brown Sheep Wildfoote, 75% wool/25% nylon, 1.75 oz (50g)/ 215 yd (197m) skeins 1 skein mc Blue Flannel/#SY 28 1 skein cc1 Blue Blood Red/#SY 26 1 skein cc2 Rock 'n' Roll/#SY 100 **Note:** Left sock uses red alternating with the variegated yarn; right sock uses blue with the variegated.) **Worsted-Weight Version (not shown)** Cascade 220, 100% wool, 3.5 oz (100g)/220 yd (202m) skeins 1 skein mc solid color 1 skein cc1 solid color 1 skein cc2 solid or multicolor
Needles	**Fingering-Weight Version:** One 5-needle set US #1 (2.25mm) double-point needles, *or size you need to obtain correct gauge* **Worsted-Weight Version:** One 5-needle set US #3 (3.25mm) double-point needles, *or size you need to obtain correct gauge*
Gauge	**Fingering-Weight Version:** 36 sts = 4" (10cm) in stockinette stitch **Worsted-Weight Version:** 24 sts = 4" (10cm) in stockinette stitch
Other supplies	Tape measure, yarn needle, needle and stitch gauge
Abbreviations	**cc** = contrasting color; **K** = knit; **K2tog** = knit 2 stitches together; **mc** = main color; **P** = purl; **P2tog** = purl 2 stitches together; **rs** = right side; **ssk** = slip, slip, knit the 2 slipped stitches together; **st(s)** = stitches; **ws** = wrong side

GETTING STARTED	FINGERING WT	WORSTED WT
Note: You may adjust the leg, heel, and/or foot lengths by working more or fewer rounds, as desired. Rounds begin and end on the right-hand side of the sock as worn. This means color changes will be made at the right-hand side, too, and Needles 1 and 2 will be the instep needles.		
Setup: With cc1, loosely cast on	70 sts	50 sts
Divide the stitches among the 4 needles as follows:		
Needle 1:	20 sts	15 sts
Needle 2:	15 sts	10 sts
Needle 3:	20 sts	15 sts
Needle 4:	15 sts	10 sts
Join into a round, being careful not to twist stitches. (For instructions, see Joining: Trading Places and Getting Ready to Work, page 16.)		
WORKING THE RIBBING		
Rounds 1–8: Work K1, P1 (ribbing) to end of each round. Measurement from cast-on edge will be about	¾" (2cm)	1¼" (3cm)
Round 9: Continuing with cc1, knit to end of round. Break off cc1, leaving a tail to weave in.		
Round 10: With mc, knit to end of round.		
Round 11: Purl to end of round. (Do not break mc.)		
WORKING THE SOCK LEG		
Note: The Checkered Textures Pattern Stitch you are establishing in the next 4 rounds is a multiple of 10 stitches and 8 rows. Two rounds of cc2 alternate with two rounds of mc in this pattern.		
Round 1: Using cc2, *K5, P5; repeat from * to end of round.		
Round 2: Using cc2, knit to end of round.		
Round 3: Using mc, *K5, P5; repeat from * to end of round.		
Round 4: Using mc, knit to end of round.		

	FINGERING WT	WORSTED WT
Round 5: Using cc2, *P5, K5; repeat from * to end of round.		
Round 6: Using cc2, knit to end of round.		
Round 7: Using mc, *P5, K5; repeat from * to end of round.		
Round 8: Using mc, knit to end of round.		
Next Rounds: Repeat Rounds 1–8 until sock leg measures 7" (17.5cm) from cast-on edge. Stretch a bit vertically and horizontally when measuring, because the textured pattern compacts. End leg by working an odd-numbered round. Break off mc and cc2, leaving tails for weaving in. **Hint:** Make a note of the last round worked in order to be able to continue the pattern across the instep after making the heel.		
MAKING THE HEEL FLAP		
Note: Slip stitches purlwise when making the heel flap and turning the heel, holding yarn in front on wrong-side rows and yarn in back on right-side rows.		
The instep stitches are held aside on Needles 1 and 2 while you work the heel flap. The instep contains	35 sts	25 sts
The heel stitches are worked back and forth using 2 needles. The heel contains	35 sts	25 sts
Setup: Turn last needle worked (Needle 4) over to wrong side to begin heel flap.		
Row 1 (ws): Using cc1, slip 1, purl to end of row.		
Row 2 (rs): *Slip 1, K1; repeat from * to last 2 sts, then K2.		
Repeat Rows 1 and 2	17 more times	13 more times
Heel will measure about 2½" (6cm). End by working Row 2 (right side).		
TURNING THE HEEL		
Setup: Turn over to wrong side to begin.		
Row 1: Slip 1, ___, P2tog, P1, turn, leaving ___ unworked.	P19 12 sts	P13 8 sts

	FINGERING WT	WORSTED WT
Row 2: Slip 1, ___, ssk, K1, turn, leaving ___ unworked.	K6 12	K4 8
Row 3: Slip 1, ___, P2tog, P1, turn, leaving ___ unworked.	P7 10 sts	P5 6 sts
Row 4: Slip 1, ___, ssk, K1, turn, leaving ___ unworked.	K8 10 sts	K6 6 sts
Row 5: Slip 1, ___, P2tog, P1, turn, leaving ___ unworked.	P9 8 sts	P7 4 sts
Row 6: Slip 1, ___, ssk, K1, turn, leaving ___ unworked.	K10 8 sts	K8 4 sts
Row 7: Slip 1, ___, P2tog, P1, turn, leaving ___ unworked.	P11 6 sts	P9 2 sts
Row 8: Slip 1, ___, ssk, K1, turn, leaving ___ unworked.	K12 6 sts	K10 2 sts
Row 9: Slip 1, ___, P2tog, P1, turn, leaving ___ unworked.	P13 4 sts	P11 0 sts
Row 10: Slip 1, ___, ssk, K1, turn, leaving ___ unworked.	K14 4 sts	K12 0 sts
Worsted Weight only: Heel turning completed. You now have		15 sts
Fingering Weight only: **Row 11:** Slip 1, ___, P2tog, P1, turn, leaving ___ unworked.	P15 2 sts	
Row 12: Slip 1, ___, ssk, K1, turn, leaving ___ unworked.	K16 2 sts	
Row 13: Slip 1, ___, P2tog, P1, turn, leaving ___ unworked.	P17 0 sts	
Row 14: Slip 1, ___, ssk, K1. Unworked stitches:	K18 0	
Fingering Weight only: Heel turning completed. You now have	21 sts	

	FINGERING WT	WORSTED WT
For both weights, break off cc1, leaving tail to weave in.		
PICKING UP STITCHES FOR HEEL GUSSET		
Note: Verify which pattern round was worked immediately before beginning the heel flap and be sure to work the next even-numbered round in Checkered Textures Pattern Stitch. For techniques, see Secrets for Tight, Smooth Gussets, pages 26–29.		
Setup: Change to mc and cc2 and resume alternating mc and cc2 as established on leg.		
Using needle with remaining heel stitches, pick up and knit ___ along right side of heel flap.	19 sts	15 sts
Needles 1 and 2 (instep): Work the appropriate even-numbered round in Checkered Textures Pattern Stitch across Needles 1 and 2 (instep stitches).		
Needle 3 (empty): Pick up and knit ___ along left side of heel flap.	19 sts	15 sts
Onto same Needle 3, knit ___ from heel stitches.	10 sts	7 sts
Needle 4: Knit remaining heel stitches plus stitches picked up along right side of heel flap.		
You now have		
Needle 1:	20 sts	15 sts
Needle 2:	15 sts	10 sts
Needle 3:	30 sts	23 sts
Needle 4:	29 sts	22 sts
Total on all 4 needles:	94 sts	70 sts
WORKING THE GUSSET DECREASES		
Round 1		
Needles 1 and 2: Work established Checkered Textures Pattern.		
Needle 3: K1, ssk, K to end of needle.		
Needle 4: Knit to last 3 sts, K2tog, K1.		
Round 2		
Needles 1 and 2: Work established Checkered Textures Pattern.		
Needles 3 and 4: Knit to end of each needle.		

	FINGERING WT	WORSTED WT
Next Rounds: Repeat Rounds 1 and 2 until you have a total of	70 sts	50 sts
Note: Since the number of decreases needed to reach the original number of stitches is an odd number, decrease only on Needle 3 in the last round.		
WORKING THE SOCK FOOT		
Next Rounds: Continue to work in established Checkered Textures Pattern Stitch, *but make no further decreases,* until measurement from back of heel is 1½" (4cm) less than desired sock length. (See Making a More Blunt, Rounded Toe, page 75.)		
SHAPING THE TOE		
Setup: Break off both mc and cc2, leaving tails to weave in. Work toe in cc1.		
Round 1 Needle 1: K1, ssk, K to end of needle. Needle 2: Knit to last 3 sts, K2tog, K1. Needle 3: K1, ssk, K to end of needle. Needle 4: Knit to last 3 sts, K2tog, K1.		
Round 2: Knit to end of each needle.		
Repeat Rounds 1 and 2	6 more times	3 more times
You now have	42 sts	34 sts
Work Round 1 every round until you have	14 sts	10 sts
CLOSING THE TOE AND FINISHING THE SOCK		
Setup: Slip the Needle 1 and 2 stitches onto one needle and the Needle 3 and 4 stitches onto another needle. On each of the 2 needles you now have	7 sts	5 sts
Graft front and back stitches together using Kitchener stitch. (For instructions, see pages 29–30.)		

	FINGERING WT	WORSTED WT
Weave in end after grafting toe. Weave in any other loose ends.		
To block, lightly mist or steam sock and pat into shape.		

Easy Pick Up

You can use just the right-hand needle to pick up and knit the stitches along the edge of the heel flap, as shown below. Or, if you prefer, use either of the following tools. The second is one of my favorites, and it's one that new sock knitters catch onto very quickly.

- A crochet hook
- One double-point needle used as a "helper" to find the place for the other needle to pick up the new stitch

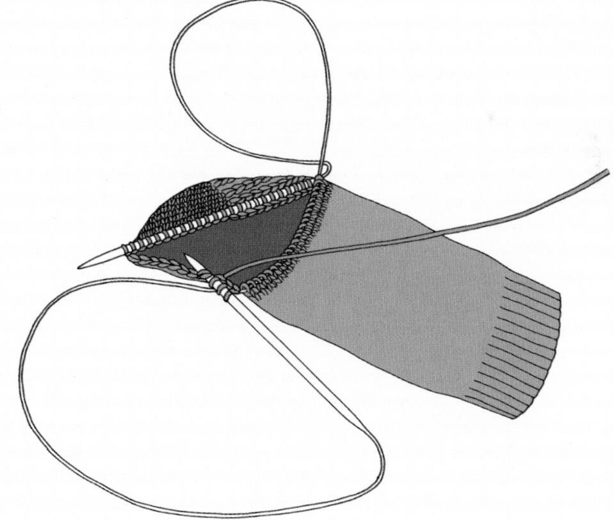

Classy Slip-Up

Slipped stitches highlight the changes in multicolored yarns and enliven solid colors on these unisex socks. They can be knit in either sport- or fingering-weight yarns. The stitch pattern is easy to memorize, and the alternating rows of stockinette and reverse stockinette rib between the slipped stitches create a cozy sock with thermal warmth.

Size	Woman's large/Man's medium
Yarn	**Fingering-Weight Version (shown at right)** Lorna's Laces Shepherd Sock Yarn, 80% superwash wool/20% nylon, 1.75 oz (54g)/215 yd (197m) skeins 2 skeins Douglas Fir **Sport-Weight Version (shown on page 53)** Mountain Colors Bearfoot, 60% superwash wool/25% mohair/ 15% nylon, 3.5 oz (100g)/350 yd (320m) skeins 1 skein Juniper
Needles	**Fingering-Weight Version:** One 5-needle set US #1 (2.25mm) double-point needles, *or size you need to obtain correct gauge* **Sport-Weight Version:** One 5-needle set US #2 (2.75mm) double-point needles, *or size you need to obtain correct gauge*
Gauge	**Fingering-Weight Version:** 32 sts = 4" (10cm) in stockinette stitch **Sport-Weight Version:** 28 sts = 4" (10cm) in stockinette stitch
Other supplies	Tape measure, yarn needle, needle-and-stitch gauge
Abbreviations	**K**= knit; **K2tog** = knit 2 stitches together; **P** = purl; **P2tog** = purl 2 stitches together; **rs** = right side; **rnd(s)** = rounds; **ssk** = slip, slip, knit the 2 slipped stitches together; **st(s)** = stitch(es); **ws** = wrong side; **wyb** = with yarn in back

GETTING STARTED	FINGERING WT	SPORT WT
Setup: Cast on	68 sts	56 sts
Divide stitches among 4 needles, as follows:		
Needle 1 (instep):	16 sts	12 sts
Needle 2 (instep):	16 sts	16 sts
Needle 3 (heel):	16 sts	12 sts
Needle 4 (heel):	20 sts	16 sts
Join into a round, being careful not to twist stitches. (For instructions, see Joining: Trading Places and Getting Ready to Work, page 16.)		
WORKING THE RIBBING AND SOCK LEG		
Ribbing: K1, P1 to end of each round until measurement from cast-on edge is about 1½" (4cm), or for	18 rnds	14 rnds
Note: The Slipped Stitch Pattern that follows in Rounds 1–4 is worked on the leg and the instep (in a modified version) down to the toe shaping. It is a multiple of 4 stitches and 4 rounds. The beginning and end of each round will be on the right-hand side of the foot.		
Round 1: Knit to end of each needle.		
Round 2: P1, *slip 1 purlwise wyb, P3; repeat from *, ending with slip 1 wyb, P2.		
Round 3: P1, *K1, P3; repeat from *, ending with K1, P2.		
Round 4: K1, *slip 1 purlwise wyb, K3; repeat from *, ending with slip 1 wyb, K2.		
Repeat Rounds 1–4 until sock measures 7" (17.5cm) from cast-on edge, or approximately	20 times	16 times
End by completing Round 4. Stretch out sock a bit vertically and horizontally when measuring, as this horizontally ribbed pattern tends to "scrunch up."		

MAKING A TRADITIONAL FRENCH HEEL	FINGERING WT	SPORT WT
Note: The *Fingering Weight* version has more instep stitches than heel stitches, and the *Sport Weight* version has more heel than instep stitches. This is done to center the pattern across the instep. For a custom fit, you can work more or fewer rows for a longer or shorter heel flap. While working heel flap and turning the heel, slip all slipped stitches purlwise, with yarn in front for wrong-side rows and yarn in back for right-side rows.		
Setup: To prepare for heel flap, rearrange stitches as follows: *Fingering Weight only:* Transfer 3 stitches from Needle 3 (heel) to Needle 2 (instep).		
Needle 1:	16 sts	
Needle 2:	19 sts	
Needle 3:	13 sts	
Needle 4:	20 sts	
For the instep, you now have	35 sts	
For the heel, you now have	33 sts	
Total on all 4 needles:	68 sts	
Sport Weight only: Transfer 1 stitch from Needle 2 (instep) to Needle 3 (heel).		
Needle 1:		12 sts
Needle 2:		15 sts
Needle 3:		13 sts
Needle 4:		16 sts
For the instep, you now have		27 sts
For the heel, you now have		29 sts
Total on all 4 needles:		56 sts
Both weights: Transfer Needle 3 stitches to Needle 4. Turn last needle used (Needle 4) around to wrong side so that you begin to work across wrong side of heel stitches. You will work back and forth using 2 needles. The heel has	33 sts	29 sts
Row 1 (ws): Slip 1, purl to end of needle, turn.		
Row 2 (rs): *Slip 1, K1; repeat from * across row to last st, K1.		

	FINGERING WT	SPORT WT
Repeat Rows 1 and 2 until heel is approximately 2½" (6cm), *or* End at the completion of a right-side row (Row 2).	16 more times	13 more times
TURNING THE HEEL		
Turn, to begin working the heel turning on the wrong side.		
Row 1: Slip 1, ___, P2tog, P1, turn, leaving ___ unworked.	P17 12 sts	P15 10 sts
Row 2: Slip 1, K4, ssk, K1, turn to ws, leaving ___ unworked.	12 sts	10 sts
Row 3: Slip 1, P5, P2tog, P1, turn, leaving ___ unworked.	10 sts	8 sts
Row 4: Slip 1, K6, ssk, K1, turn, leaving ___ unworked.	10 sts	8 sts
Row 5: Slip 1, P7, P2tog, P1, turn, leaving ___ unworked.	8 sts	6 sts
Row 6: Slip 1, K8, ssk, K1, turn, leaving ___ unworked.	8 sts	6 sts
Row 7: Slip 1, P9, P2tog, P1, turn, leaving ___ unworked.	6 sts	4 sts
Row 8: Slip 1, K10, ssk, K1, turn, leaving ___ unworked.	6 sts	4 sts
Row 9: Slip 1, P11, P2tog, P1, turn, leaving ___ unworked.	4 sts	2 sts
Row 10: Slip 1, K12, ssk, K1, turn, leaving ___ unworked.	4 sts	2 sts
Row 11: Slip 1, P13, P2tog, P1, turn, leaving ___ unworked.	2 sts	0 sts
Row 12: Slip 1, K14, ssk, K1, leaving ___ unworked.	2 sts	0 sts
Sport Weight only: Turning complete. (Skip Rows 13 and 14.) You now have		17 sts
Fingering Weight only: **Row 13:** Slip 1, P15, P2tog, P1, turn, leaving ____ unworked.	0 sts	
Row 14: Slip 1, K16, ssk, K1. Turning complete. You now have	19 sts	

PICKING UP STITCHES FOR HEEL GUSSET	FINGERING WT	SPORT WT
Note: In this section, you will be working with only 4 needles (3 with stitches, and 1 empty). The Slipped Stitch Pattern in this section has been modified for the instep. For techniques, see Secrets for Tight, Smooth Gussets, pages 26–29.		
Setup:		
Using the empty needle, pick up and knit ___ along right side of heel flap.	18 sts	15 sts
Needle 1: Knit all of the instep stitches onto a single needle. For the instep, you will have	35 sts	27 sts
Needle 2: With empty needle, pick up and knit ___ along left side of heel flap.	18 sts	15 sts
Also with this needle, knit ___ from next needle.	9 sts	9 sts
Needle 3: With empty needle knit ___ remaining heel stitches.	10	8
Also with this needle, knit the ___ picked up from the right side of the heel flap.	18 sts	15 sts
You now have		
Needle 1 (instep):	35 sts	27 sts
Needle 2 (heel):	27 sts	24 sts
Needle 3 (heel):	28 sts	23 sts
Total on all 4 needles:	90 sts	74 sts

WORKING GUSSET DECREASES

Round 1

Needle 1: P1, *slip 1 wyb, P3; repeat from *, ending with slip 1 wyb, P1.

Needle 2: K1, ssk, K to end of needle.

Needle 3: Knit to last 3 sts, K2tog, K1.

Round 2

Needle 1: P1, *K1, P3; repeat from *, ending with K1, P1.

Needle 2: Knit to end of needle.

Needle 3: Knit to end of needle.

	FINGERING WT	SPORT WT
Round 3 Needle 1: K1, *slip 1 wyb, K3; repeat from *, ending with slip 1 wyb, K1. Needle 2: K1, ssk, K to end of needle. Needle 3: Knit to last 3 sts, K2tog, K1.		
Round 4: Knit to end of each needle.		
Repeat Rounds 1–4 until you have a total of	68 sts	56 sts
Finish working the gusset decreases at the end of a Round 3.		
WORKING THE SOCK FOOT		
Continue to work the pattern as established (Rounds 1–4 above), *but make no further decreases in Rounds 1 and 3.*		
End by working a Slipped Stitch Pattern Round 4 when measurement from back of heel is 1½" (4cm) less than desired length.		
Fingering Weight only: Slip last stitch of Needle 1 onto Needle 2.		
You now have		
Needle 1:	34 sts	
Needle 2 :	17 sts	
Total on all 3 needles:	68 sts	
Sport Weight only: Slip first stitch of Needle 2 to end of Needle 1.		
You now have		
Needle 1:		28 sts
Needle 2:		14 sts
Total on all 3 needles:		56 sts
SHAPING THE TOE		
Round 1 Needle 1: K1, ssk, K to last 3 sts, K2tog, K1. Needle 2: K1, ssk, K to end of needle. Needle 3: Knit to last 3 sts, K2tog, K1.		

	FINGERING WT	SPORT WT
Round 2: Knit to end of each needle.		
Next Rounds: Repeat Rounds 1 and 2	5 more times	4 more times
You now have	44 sts	36 sts
Next Round: Repeat Round 1 (decrease round) every round until you have	16 sts	16 sts
CLOSING THE TOE AND FINISHING THE SOCK		
In preparation for closing the toe, slip all the heel stitches onto one needle and hold parallel to instep stitches needle. Graft front and back stitches together using Kitchener stitch. (For instructions, see pages 29–30.)		
Weave in end after grafting toe. Weave in any other loose ends.		
To block, lightly mist or steam sock and pat into shape.		

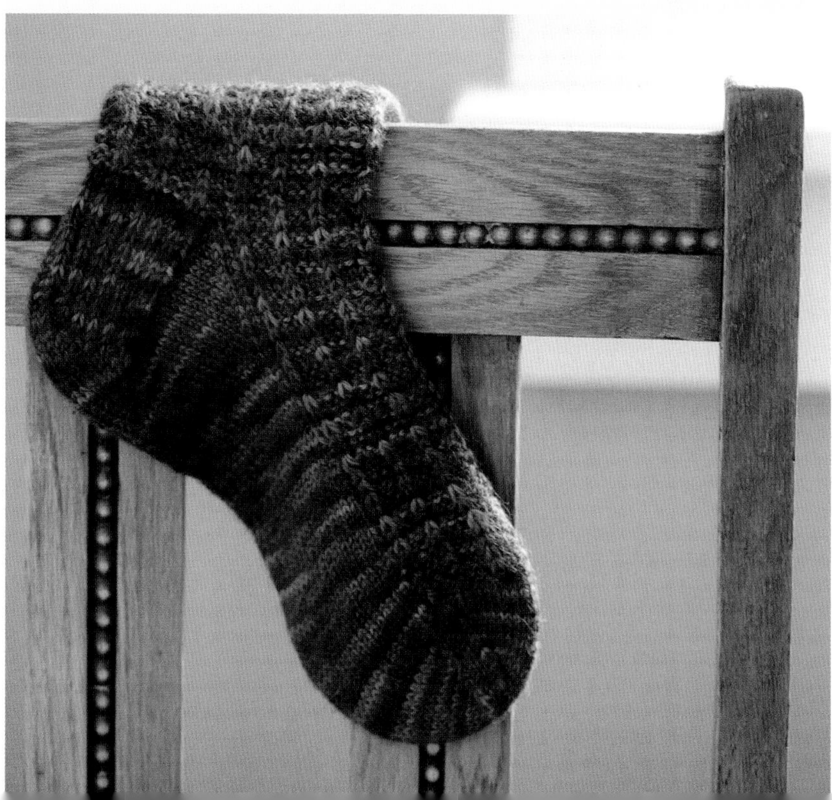

Winter Garden

Lace edging tops a traditional Estonian patterned cuff paired with lively stripes, for a sock that is fun to knit and fun to wear. The color pattern on the cuff provides another opportunity to try two-color stranding. For variety, knit the entire cuff in lace by continuing it to the desired length. This pattern was inspired by socks designed by Nancy Bush.

Size	Woman's medium–large
Yarn	Louet Gems Super Fine #1, fingering weight, 100% merino wool, 1.75 oz (50g)/185 yd (170m) skeins 1 skein mc #39 (fern green) 1 skein cc1 #30 (cream) 1 skein cc2 #87 (mint) **Note:** In the pair shown, the blue and green are reversed in the patterning and striping of the second sock for fun and interest. That is, the mc is changed to mint and cc2 to fern green. Enough yarn will be left to make striped socks for a child.
Needles	One 5-needle set US #1.5 (2.5mm) double-point needles, *or size you need to obtain correct gauge* Plus, *if needed to maintain same gauge in the stranded sections*, one 5-needle set US #2 (2.75mm) double-point needles
Gauge	28 sts = 4" (10cm) in stockinette stitch
Other supplies	Tape measure, yarn needle, needle and stitch gauge, stitch markers
Abbreviations	**cc** = contrasting color; **K** = knit; **K2tog** = knit 2 stitches together; **mc** = main color; **P** = purl; **P2tog** = purl 2 stitches together; **psso** = pass slipped stitch over; **rs** = right side; **ssk** = slip, slip, knit the 2 slipped stitches together; **st(s)** = stitch(es); **ws** = wrong side; **wyb** = with yarn in back; **YO** = yarn over

GETTING STARTED

Setup: Using smaller needles and cc1, loosely cast on 64 stitches. Divide evenly among needles. There will be 32 instep and 32 heel stitches. Join into a round, being careful not to twist stitches. (For instructions, see Joining: Trading Places and Getting Ready to Work, page 16.)

Note: Rounds for the sock leg start and end on the right-hand side of the sock as worn. After turning the heel, rounds for the sole and toe of the sock start and end on the bottom of the sock.

Round 1: Knit to end of round.

Round 2: Purl to end of round.

Round 3: Knit to end of round.

WORKING THE SCALLOPED LACE EDGING

You begin to work the Scalloped Lace Pattern in the next round. This pattern is a multiple of 8 stitches and 2 rows. You work 4 pattern repeats on both the heel and instep stitches.
Hint: You may wish to use stitch markers or coilless safety pins to separate pattern repeats.

Round 1: *P1, slip 1 wyb knitwise, K1, psso, K1, YO, K1, YO, K1, K2tog; repeat from * to end of round.

Round 2: *P1, K7; repeat from * to end of round.

Rounds 3–6: Repeat Rounds 1 and 2. If you'd prefer a longer edging, you can work additional rounds.

Round 7: Purl to end of round. Change to larger needles if needed to maintain gauge in the stranded knitting sections.

WORKING THE WINTER GARDEN CHART

Using cc1 and, if needed for gauge, the larger needles, follow the Winter Garden Cuff Chart (top of page 63), working from right to left and starting on Line 1 at the bottom. Add mc and cc2 as called for in the chart and in the written directions below. (The round numbers correspond with chart line numbers.)

Round 1: Using cc1, knit all sts.

Round 2: Using cc2 and cc1, *K3 cc2, K5 cc1; repeat from * to end of round.

Round 3: Using cc2 and cc1, *K4 cc2, K1 cc1, K1 cc2, K1 cc1, K1 cc2; repeat from * to end of round.

Round 4: Using cc2 and cc1, *K1 cc2, K1 cc1, K2 cc2, K3 cc1, K1 cc2; repeat from * to end of round.

Round 5: Using cc2 and cc1, *K4 cc2, K1 cc1, K1 cc2, K1 cc1, K1 cc2; repeat from * to end of round.

Round 6: Using cc2 and cc1, *K3 cc2, K5 cc1; repeat from * to end of round.

Round 7: Using cc1 and mc, *K4 cc1, K3 mc, K1 cc1; repeat from * to end of round.

Round 8: Using cc1 and mc, *K1 cc1, K1 mc, K1 cc1, K5 mc; repeat from * to end of round.

Round 9: Using cc1 and mc, *K3 cc1, K2 mc, K1 cc1, K2 mc; repeat from * to end of round.

Round 10: Using cc1 and mc, *K1 cc1, K1 mc, K1 cc1, K5 mc; repeat from * to end of round.

Round 11: Using cc1 and mc, *K4 cc1, K3 mc, K1 cc1; repeat from * to end of round. Break off mc, leaving a 6" (15cm) tail to weave in.

Rounds 12–16: Repeat Rounds 2–6. At the end of Round 16, break off cc2, leaving a 6" (15cm) tail to weave in.

Round 17: Using cc1, knit to end of round. If using larger needle for stranded knitting on cuff, switch back to smaller needles now.

Round 18: Using cc1 and smaller needles, purl to end of round. Break off cc1, leaving a 6" (15cm) tail to weave in.

KNITTING THE STRIPED LEG

Note: The stockinette-stitch leg features alternating stripes of mc and cc2. For a little surprise and visual interest, the stripe size changes from 4 to 5 rows of each color midway down the sock foot. For an easy technique for smoothing out the "jog" where colors change in stripes, see Striping without Jogs, page 58.

Rounds 1–4: Using mc, knit to end of each round.

Rounds 5–8: Using cc2, knit to end of each round.

Striping without Jogs

When knitting in the round, rather than producing completed circles, you are actually knitting an ever-moving spiral. This results in a "jog," or little step up, when the first stitch of the new color's second row is knit. Meg Swansen popularized a simple "jogless join" technique to avoid this problem and to smooth out the transition from one color to another. Here's how to do it:

1. When you are ready to add a new yarn, drop the old yarn and knit the first stitch in the round with the new yarn.
2. Knit a complete round with the new yarn.
3. Just before you knit the first stitch of the second round of the new yarn, use the tip of your right-hand needle to reach down below the first new yarn stitch into the old yarn stitch under it, and lift the right leg of the old stitch onto the left-hand needle.
4. Knit the old and new stitches together, then continue working with the new yarn.

You do this "jogless join" only one time when you are changing colors and are ready to begin the second round of the new color. When you later weave in the tails, pull them to tighten as usual and then weave them into the wrong side. Weave in a direction that helps pull the old yarn up and the new yarn down a bit to further smooth out the join. For more advice on starting new yarns, see Splicing Ends Together, page 123.

Rounds 9–32: Repeat Rounds 1–8. You will have a total of 4 stripes of each color, and the leg will measure about 6½" (16cm) from the top of the scallop. End the row on the right-hand side of the leg. Break off mc and cc2, leaving 6" (15cm) tails for weaving in.

MAKING THE PATTERNED HEEL FLAP

Note: In this section you will be working back and forth on the 31 heel flap stitches, using 2 needles/needle tips, while the 33 instep stitches wait until needed again. The heel flap features a garter stitch edging, formed by knitting 3 stitches at the beginning and end of every row. Although you may want to change to the larger needle for the heel, staying on smaller needle will make heel flap tighter and give it extra durability.

Chart Notes: For the heel flap, follow the Winter Garden Heel Chart (page 63), beginning at the bottom right on Row 1. Knit all stitches on the right side (odd-numbered rows) and, except for the garter stitch edging, purl the stitches on the wrong side (even-numbered rows). The text on the next page corresponds to the chart.

Row 1 (rs): With cc1, knit across the next 31 stitches, knitting them onto 1 needle, and place the last (thirty-second) stitch on the instep needle. You now have 31 stitches on one needle, and those will be worked in the charted pattern for the heel flap. Turn to wrong side.

Row 2 (ws): K3, P25, K3, turn.

Row 3: K6 cc1, *K3 cc2, K5 cc1; repeat from * one more time; K3 cc2, K6 cc1.

Row 4: K3 cc1, P2 cc1, *P5 cc2, P1 cc1, P1 cc2, P1 cc1; repeat from * 1 more time; P5 cc2, P2 cc1, K3 cc1.

Row 5: K5 cc1, *K2 cc2, K1 cc1, K2 cc2, K3 cc1; repeat from * to last 2 stitches, K2 cc1.

Row 6: K3 cc1, P2 cc1, *P5 cc2, P1 cc1, P1 cc2, P1 cc1; repeat from * 1 more time; P5 cc2, P2 cc1, K3 cc1.

Row 7: K6 cc1, *K3 cc2, K5 cc1; repeat from * 1 more time; K3 cc2, K6 cc1.

Row 8: Using mc and cc1, K3 cc1, P7 cc1, *P3 mc, P5 cc1; repeat from * 1 more time; P2 cc1, K3 cc1.

Row 9: K7 cc1, *K1 mc, K1 cc1, K5 mc, K1 cc1; repeat from * 1 more time; K1 mc, K7 cc1.

Row 10: K3 cc1, P6 cc1, *P2 mc, P1 cc1, P2 mc, P3 cc1; repeat from * 1 more time; P3 cc1, K3 cc1.

Row 11: K7 cc1, *K1 mc, K1 cc1, K5 mc, K1 cc1; repeat from * 1 more time; K1 mc, K7 cc1.

Row 12: K3 cc1, P7 cc1, P3 mc, P5 cc1, P3 mc, P7 cc1, K3 cc1. Break off mc, leaving a 6" (15cm) tail for weaving in.

Rows 13–17: Using cc1 and cc2, repeat Rows 3–7. Break off cc2, leaving a 6" (15cm) tail for weaving in.

Rows 18 and 20 (ws): Using cc1, K3, P25, K3.

Rows 19 and 21 (rs): Knit to end of each row.

Next Rows: Repeat Rows 18 and 19 until heel flap measures 2½" (6cm), or desired length. End by working a right-side row in preparation for turning the heel. If using a larger needle, switch back to smaller needles now.

TURNING THE HEEL

Note: Begin the heel turning on the wrong side. Slip all stitches purlwise with yarn in front on wrong-side rows and with yarn in back on right-side rows.

Row 1: Using cc1 and the smaller needles, slip 1, P17, P2tog, P1, turn, leaving 10 sts unworked.

Row 2: Slip 1, K6, ssk, K1, turn, leaving 10 sts.

Row 3: Slip 1, P7, P2tog, P1, turn, leaving 8 sts.

Row 4: Slip 1, K8, ssk, K1, turn, leaving 8 sts.

Row 5: Slip 1, P9, P2tog, P1, turn, leaving 6 sts.

Row 6: Slip 1, K10, ssk, K1, turn, leaving 6 sts.

Row 7: Slip 1, P11, P2tog, P1, turn, leaving 4 sts.

Row 8: Slip 1, K12, ssk, K1, turn, leaving 4 sts.

Row 9: Slip 1, P13, P2tog, P1, turn, leaving 2 sts.

Row 10: Slip 1, K14, ssk, K1, turn, leaving 2 sts.

Row 11: Slip 1, P15, P2tog, P1, turn, leaving 0 sts.

Row 12: Slip 1, K16, ssk, K1, turn, leaving 0 sts. Heel turning complete. You have 19 stitches. Cut cc1, leaving a 6" (15cm) tail for weaving in. Weave in ends on flap.

PICKING UP STITCHES FOR HEEL GUSSET

Note: For techniques, see Secrets for Tight, Smooth Gusssets, pages 26–29.

Setup

Using mc and same needle/needle tip (needle with remaining heel stitches), pick up and knit 15 stitches along right side of heel. If you are using double points, this will be Needle 1 (heel).

Knit all instep stitches (Needles 2 and 3).

Pick up and knit 15 stitches along left side of heel (this becomes Needle 4). On same needle, knit 9 remaining heel stitches from Needle 1.

You now have

Needle 1 (heel): 25 stitches

Needle 2 (instep): 17 stitches

Needle 3 (instep): 16 stitches

Needle 4 (heel): 24 stitches

Total on all 4 needles: 82 stitches

Note: Rounds begin and end in center back and sole. As you work the gusset decreases, you will also be working alternating 4-round stripes of mc and cc2.

Round 1

Needle 1: Knit to last 3 sts, K2tog, K1.

Needles 2 and 3: Knit to end of each needle.

Needle 4: K1, ssk, K to end of needle.

Round 2: Knit to end of each needle.

Repeat Rounds 1 and 2 until 64 stitches remain. Gusset is complete; make no further decreases.

You now have

Needle 1: 16 stitches

Needle 2: 17 stitches

Needle 3: 16 stitches

Needle 4: 15 stitches

Total on all 4 needles: 64 stitches

Socks of Another Stripe

Varying the number of stripes on the leg and the foot is a way to change the sock length and size. If desired, you can end the sock toe without having just a few rows of a new color. To do this, continue working your last color a few more rounds to complete the sock, including running a tail through the final stitches to close the toe. For example, the sock pictured on page 55 has a final color segment of 8 rounds, a few more than the 5-round striping sequence used in the foot.

WORKING THE SOCK FOOT

Rounds 1–24: Knit to the end of each round, continuing the 4-round striping pattern as established. You will have 3 pairs of mc and cc2 stripes.

Next Rounds: Begin working 5-round stripes, maintaining the same alternating color pattern, until sock measures 8¼" (21cm) from back of heel, or desired length to beginning of toe shaping.

SHAPING THE ROUND TOE

Setup: If using double-point needles, slip 1 stitch from Needle 2 (instep) to Needle 3 (instep) and 1 stitch from Needle 3 (instep) to Needle 4 (heel).You now have all instep stitches together on a needle/needle tip and all heel stitches together on another needle/needle tip. Continue the striping pattern as established.

Round 1: *K6, K2tog; repeat from * to end of round. You now have 56 stitches.

Rounds 2–3: Knit to end of each round.

Round 4: *K5, K2tog; repeat from * to end of round. You now have 48 stitches.

Rounds 5–6: Knit to end of each round.

Round 7: *K4, K2tog; repeat from * to end of round. You now have 40 stitches.

Rounds 8–9: Knit to end of each round.

Round 10: *K3, K2tog; repeat from * to end of round. You now have 32 stitches.

Rounds 11–12: Knit to end of each round.

Round 13: *K2, K2tog; repeat from * to end of round. You now have 24 stitches.

Rounds 14–15: Knit to end of each round.

Round 16: *K1, K2tog; repeat from * to end of round. You now have 16 stitches.

Round 17: K2tog to end of round. You now have 8 stitches.

CLOSING THE TOE AND FINISHING THE SOCK

Break off yarn leaving a 8" (20cm) tail, thread tail through yarn needle, and run yarn through remaining 8 stitches. Draw stitches together, tighten, take yarn through to wrong side, and weave in.

To block, lightly mist or steam sock and pat into shape. Blocking will help smooth out your stranded Fair Isle patterning.

Winter Garden Cuff Chart (work in the round)

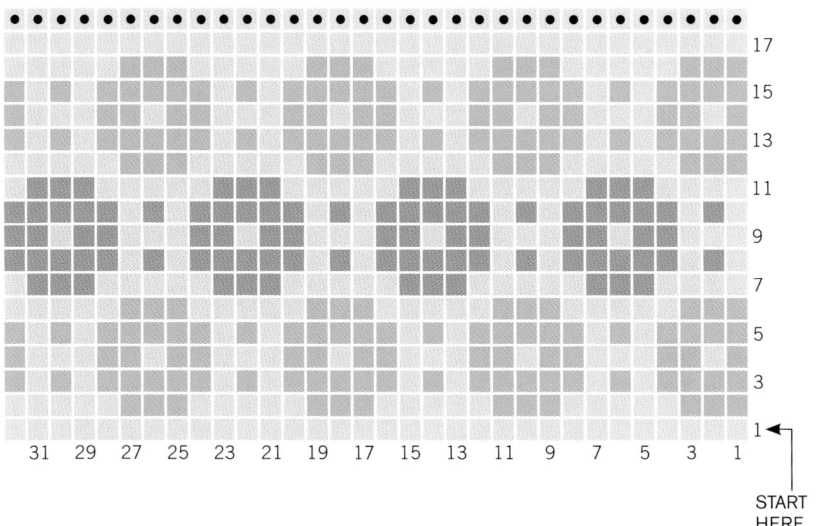

Winter Garden Heel Chart (work from side to side)

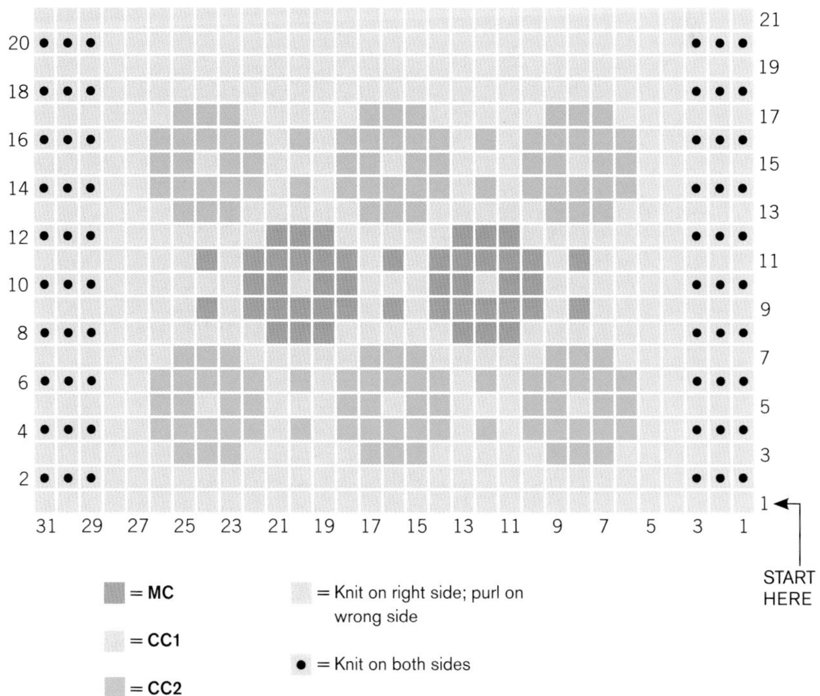

= MC

= CC1

= CC2

= Knit on right side; purl on wrong side

● = Knit on both sides

Little Guys

Knitting these cute toddler-sized socks is like eating popcorn – once you start it's hard to stop! Use your imagination to create your own signature gifts. Combine leftover yarns to make socks with several colors.

Size	Toddler (18–24 mo.) Model is 4¾" (12cm) long; to change size, work more or fewer rows for the foot.
Yarn	Dalegarn Baby Ull, 100% wool, fingering weight, 1.75 oz (50g)/ 190 yd (174m) skeins **Single Strand Version** *(1 skein is enough for 2 pairs toddler socks):* 1 skein Baby Ull #4711 (light pink) *or* 1 skein Baby Ull #5701 (light blue) *or* 1 skein Baby Ull #0010 (white) *or* 1 skein Baby Ull #2203 (light yellow) **Double Strand Version** *(1 skein is enough for 1 pair and a spare toddler sock)* 1 skein Baby Ull #9013 (light green)
Needles	One 5-needle set of double-point needles as follows, *or size you need to obtain correct gauge:* **Single Strand Version:** US #1 or 1.5 (2.25mm or 2.50mm) **Double Strand Version:** US #3 (3.25mm)
Gauge	**Single Strand Version:** 32 sts = 4" (10cm) worked with 1 strand in stockinette stitch **Double Strand Version:** 24 sts = 4" (10cm) worked with 2 strands in stockinette stitch
Other supplies	Tape measure, yarn needle, needle and stitch gauge
Abbreviations	**K** = knit; **K2tog** = knit 2 stitches together; **P** = purl; **P2tog** = purl 2 stitches together; **rs** = right side; **rnd(s)** = round(s); **ssk** = slip, slip, knit the 2 slipped stitches together; **st(s)** = stitch(es); **ws** = wrong side; **wyb** = with the yarn in back; **wyf** = with the yarn in front

GETTING STARTED	SINGLE STRAND	DOUBLE STRAND
Note: The rounds in this sock start and end at the right-hand side of the foot.		
Setup: Loosely cast on	40 sts	32 sts
Divide stitches evenly among 4 needles. Each double-point needle will have	10 sts	8 sts
Note: If you are using circular needles, you will have 20 instep stitches and 20 heel/sole stitches for *Single Strand* sock, and 16 instep stitches and 16 heel/sole stitches for *Double Strand* sock. Join into a round, being careful not to twist stitches. (For instructions, see Joining: Trading Places and Getting Ready to Work, page 16.)		
WORKING THE RIBBING		
Work in K1, P1 ribbing for	12 rnds (about 1½"/4cm)	10 rnds (about 1¼"/3cm)
KNITTING THE SOCK LEG		
Round 1: P1, *K2, P2; repeat from * to end of each needle, ending with P1.		
Round 2: Knit to end of each needle.		
Repeat Rounds 1 and 2 (Broken Rib Stitch Pattern) for 1¾" (4.375cm) for the leg (not including cuff), or until desired length to beginning of heel.		
End leg by working Round 1 one more time.		
MAKING THE HEEL FLAP		
Note: The heel flap is worked back and forth on 2 needles. The remaining stitches (instep stitches) wait on Needles 1 and 2 until you use them again in Picking Up Stitches for Heel Gusset (page 68). Start working on the wrong side. The heel flap has	20 sts	16 sts
Row 1: Slip 1 purlwise wyf, purl to end of needle, turn over to rs.		
Row 2: *Slip 1 purlwise wyb, K1; repeat from * to end of needle, turn over to ws.		

	SINGLE STRAND	DOUBLE STRAND
Repeat Rows 1 and 2	9 more times	7 more times
Heel flap will be approximately	1½" (4cm)	1½" (4cm)
TURNING THE HEEL		
NOTE: Begin turning the heel on the wrong side, slipping all slipped stitches purlwise with yarn in front on wrong-side rows and in back on right-side rows.		
Row 1 (ws): Slip 1, ____, P2tog, P1, turn, leaving ____ unworked.	P10 6 sts	P8 4 sts
Row 2 (rs): Slip 1, K3, ssk, K1, turn, leaving ___ unworked.	6 sts	4 sts
Row 3: Slip 1, P4, P2tog, P1, turn, leaving ___ unworked.	4 sts	2 sts
Row 4: Slip 1, K5, ssk, K1, turn, leaving ___ unworked.	4 sts	2 sts
Row 5: Slip 1, P6, P2tog, P1, turn, leaving ___ unworked.	2 sts	0 sts
Row 6: Slip 1, K7, ssk, K1, leaving ___ unworked.	2 sts	0 sts
Double Strand only: Do not turn to wrong side. Double Strand sock heel turning is complete. Break off yarn leaving a tail for weaving in. You now have		10 sts
Single Strand only: **Row 7:** Slip 1, P8, P2tog, P1, turn, leaving ___ unworked.	0 sts	
Row 8: Slip 1, K9, ssk, K1, leaving ___ unworked.	0 sts	
Do not turn to wrong side. Heel turning is complete. Break off yarn leaving a tail for weaving in. You now have	12 sts	

PICKING UP STITCHES FOR HEEL GUSSET	SINGLE STRAND	DOUBLE STRAND
Note: If you are using 2 circular needles, remember to use the heel needle to pick up stitches along both sides of the heel flap (see Secrets for Tight, Smooth Gussets, pages 26–29).		
Setup		
Using needle with remaining heel stitches, pick up and knit ___ along right side of heel flap.	11 sts	8 sts
Needles 1 and 2: Knit to end of each needle.		
Needle 3: With empty needle, pick up and knit ___ along left side of heel flap.	11 sts	8 sts
Also on Needle 3, knit ___ from the heel stitches (half of those remaining after heel turning).	6 sts	5 sts
Needle 4: Knit to end of needle.		
You now have		
Needles 1 and 2 (instep):	10 sts	8 sts
Needles 3 and 4 (heel):	17 sts	13 sts
Total on all 4 needles:	54 sts	42 sts
WORKING GUSSET DECREASES		
Note: In this section, you will be working Broken Rib Stitch Pattern as established on Needles 1 and 2 (instep) and making the gusset decreases while knitting the stitches on Needles 3 and 4 (heel).		
Round 1		
Needle 1: P1, *K2, P2; repeat from * to last st, P1.		
Needle 2: P1, *K2, P2; repeat from * to last st, P1.		
Needle 3: K1, ssk, K to end of needle.		
Needle 4: Knit to last 3 sts, K2tog, K1.		
Total on all 4 needles:	52 sts	40 sts
Round 2: Knit to end of each needle.		
Repeat Rounds 1 and 2 until each of the 4 needles contains	10 sts	8 sts
All gusset decreases are completed. Total on all 4 needles:	40 sts	32 sts

WORKING THE SOCK FOOT	SINGLE STRAND	DOUBLE STRAND
Continue the established 2-round Broken Rib Stitch Pattern on Needles 1 and 2 (instep) and knit all stitches on Needles 3 and 4 (sole), making no further decreases, until sock foot measures 3½" (9cm) from back of heel, or desired length. **Note:** Sock is stretchy. Toe shaping adds 1¼" (3cm) in length to the measurement above. For larger sizes, add another ½"–1½" (1.5cm–4cm) before beginning toe shaping.		
SHAPING THE TOE		
Round 1 Needle 1: K1, ssk, K to end of needle. Needle 2: Knit to last 3 sts, K2tog, K1. Needle 3: K1, ssk, K to end of needle. Needle 4: Knit to last 3 sts, K2tog, K1. Total on all 4 needles:	36 sts	28 sts
Round 2: Knit all stitches.		
Continue working Rounds 1 and 2 until there are 3 stitches on each needle.		
Total on all 4 needles:	12 sts	12 sts
CLOSING THE TOE AND FINISHING THE SOCK		
Slip Needle 1 and 2 (instep) stitches onto one needle and the Needle 3 and 4 (heel or sole) stitches onto a second needle. Break yarn, leaving a 10" (25cm) tail for grafting toe closed. Graft front and back stitches together using the Kitchener stitch. (For instructions, see pages 29–30.)		
Weave in end, and any other loose ends. To block, lightly mist or steam sock and pat into shape.		

Low-Roll Sporty

A reverse stockinette stitch and roll tops make these stylish sport socks attractive enough to be seen anywhere. For a double roll look (not shown), create the second roll and shorten the sock leg length by pushing down the first roll approximately a half inch, allowing a second roll to magically appear. These socks knit up fast using two strands of fingering-weight yarn or a single strand of worsted, so you'll be able to knit up a pair to tuck in all your athletic bags.

Sizes	Woman's small–medium Woman's large/Man's medium
Yarn	Lana Grossa Meilenweit Cotton Fun, 45% cotton/42% wool/13% polyamid, fingering weight, 1.75 oz (50g)/208 yd (190m) skeins 1 skein mc Multi-color stripe/#336 Lana Grossa Meilenweit Cotton, 45% cotton/42% wool/13% polyamid, fingering weight, 1.75 oz (50g)/208 yd (190m) skeins 2 skeins cc Yellow/#43 **Note:** 1 skein of the solid yarn and 1 of the multi is enough for the smaller size. Socks are knit with yarn doubled throughout.
Needles	One 5-needle set US #3 (3.25mm) double-point needles, *or size you need to obtain correct gauge*
Gauge	24 stitches = 4" (10cm) in stockinette stitch
Other supplies	Tape measure, yarn needle, needle and stitch gauge
Abbreviations	**cc** = contrast color; **K** = knit; **K2tog** = knit 2 stitches together; **mc** = main color; **P** = purl; **P2tog** = purl 2 stitches together; **rs** = right side; **rnd(s)** = round(s); **ssk** = slip, slip, knit the 2 slipped stitches together; **st(s)** = stitch(es); **ws** = wrong side; **wyb** = with yarn in back; **wyf** = with yarn in front

GETTING STARTED	WOMAN'S S–M	WOMAN'S L/ MAN'S M
Setup: Holding 2 strands of cc together, loosely cast on	48 sts	56 sts
Divide stitches evenly among 4 needles. On each needle you now have	12 sts	14 sts
Join into a round, being careful not to twist stitches. (For instructions, see Joining: Trading Places and Getting Ready to Work, page 16.) Rounds begin and end on the right side of the sock when worn.		
MAKING THE DOUBLE ROLL CUFF		
Using 2 strands of cc, purl to end of each round for 1" (2.5cm).		
Break off 1 strand of cc, leaving a 6" (15cm) tail to weave in.		
Using 1 strand of cc and 1 strand of mc, knit to end of each round for 2½" (6cm), or desired length, to beginning of heel. For shorter leg, knit only 1½" (4cm) before beginning heel.		
MAKING THE HEEL FLAP		
Note: Hold the instep stitches aside on Needles 1 and 2 while you work the heel flap. The instep has	24 sts	28 sts
You will be working back and forth using 2 needles for the heel flap. As you work the heel, slip stitches purlwise with yarn in front on wrong-side rows and yarn in back on right-side rows.		
Setup: Slip the Needle 3 stitches onto Needle 4. You now have	24 sts	28 sts
Turn Needle 4 (heel) to wrong side to begin.		
Row 1: Slip 1, P to end of needle, turn to rs.		
Row 2: *Slip 1, K1; repeat from * to end of needle; turn to ws.		
Repeat Rows 1 and 2	12 more times	14 more times
You can work more or fewer rows for a longer or shorter heel flap. The sock shown measures	2½" (6cm)	2¾" (7cm)
End by working a right-side row.		

TURNING THE HEEL	WOMAN'S S–M	WOMAN'S L/ MAN'S M
Beginning on wrong side, turn the heel as follows, slipping all stitches purlwise wyf on wrong-side rows and wyb on right-side rows.		
Row 1 (ws): Slip 1, ___, P2tog, P1, turn, leaving ____ unworked.	P12 8 sts	P14 10 sts
Row 2 (rs): Slip 1, K3, ssk, K1, turn back to ws, leaving ____ unworked.	8 sts	10 sts
Row 3: Slip 1, P4, P2tog, P1, turn, leaving ____ unworked.	6 sts	8 sts
Row 4: Slip 1, K5, ssk, K1, turn, leaving ____ unworked.	6 sts	8 sts
Row 5: Slip 1, P6, P2tog, P1, turn, leaving ____ unworked.	4 sts	6 sts
Row 6: Slip 1, K7, ssk, K1, turn, leaving ____ unworked.	4 sts	6 sts
Row 7: Slip 1, P8, P2tog, P1, turn, leaving ____ unworked.	2 sts	4 sts
Row 8: Slip 1, K9, ssk, K1, turn, leaving ____ unworked.	2 sts	4 sts
Row 9: Slip 1, P10, P2tog, P1, turn, leaving ____ unworked.	0 sts	2 sts
Row 10: Slip 1, K11, ssk, K1, turn, leaving ____ unworked.	0 sts	2 sts
Woman's S–M only: Heel turning complete. You now have	14 sts	
Woman's L/Man's M only: **Row 11:** Slip 1, P12, P2tog, P1, turn, leaving ____ unworked.		0 sts
Row 12: Slip 1, K13, ssk, K1, leaving ____ unworked.		0 sts
Heel turning complete. You now have		16 sts
Both sizes: Last row worked is a right-side row. Do not turn.		

PICKING UP STITCHES FOR HEEL GUSSET	WOMAN'S S–M	WOMAN'S L/ MAN'S M
Note: For techniques, see Secrets for Tight, Smooth Gussets, pages 26–29.		
Setup		
Using needle with remaining heel stitches, pick up and knit ___ along right side of heel flap.	16 sts	18 sts
Needles 1 and 2: Knit to end of each needle.		
With empty needle (this becomes Needle 3), pick up and knit ___ along left side of heel flap.	16 sts	18 sts
Continuing on Needle 3, knit ___ from the remaining heel stitches.	7 sts	8 sts
Needle 4: Knit remaining heel stitches and stitches picked up along right side of the heel flap.		
You now have		
Needle 1:	12 sts	14 sts
Needle 2:	12 sts	14 sts
Needle 3:	23 sts	26 sts
Needle 4:	23 sts	26 sts
Total on all needles:	70 sts	80 sts
WORKING GUSSET DECREASES		
Round 1 Needles 1 and 2: Knit to end of each needle. Needle 3: K1, ssk, knit to end of needle. Needle 4: Knit to last 3 sts, K2tog, K1.		
Round 2: Knit to end of round.		
Repeat Rounds 1 and 2 until each needle contains	12 sts	14 sts
Total on all needles:	48 sts	56 sts
WORKING THE SOCK FOOT		
Note: You can knit fewer or more rounds to custom fit the length of the sock, if desired.		
Knit all rounds until sock measurement from back of heel is	8" (20cm)	8½" (21cm)
For contrasting toes, break off the strand of mc, leaving a tail for weaving in later and add a second strand of cc.		

SHAPING THE TOE	WOMAN'S S–M	WOMAN'S L/ MAN'S M
Round 1 Needle 1: K1, ssk, K to end of needle. Needle 2: Knit to last 3 sts, K2tog, Kl. Needle 3: K1, ssk, K to end of needle. Needle 4: Knit to last 3 sts, K2tog, Kl.		
Round 2: Knit to end of each needle.		
Repeat Rounds 1 and 2 until a total of 12 stitches remain.		
CLOSING THE TOE AND FINISHING THE SOCK		
Setup: Slip the Needle 1 and 2 stitches onto one needle and the Needle 3 and 4 stitches onto another. Break yarn, leaving a 10" (25cm) tail for closing the toe.		
Using tail, graft front and back stitches together using Kitchener stitch. (For instructions, see page 29–30.)		
Weave in end after grafting toe. Weave in any other loose ends.		
To block, lightly mist or steam sock and pat into shape.		

Making a More Blunt, Rounded Toe

For more blunt and rounded toe shaping, when the sock's foot length is 1½" (4cm) less than desired, work toe decreases until half the number of decreases have been made. Then work Round 2 (decrease round) every round instead of every other round until a total of 16 stitches remain.
For example, a 72-stitch sock will be decreased by 56 stitches down to 16 stitches before grafting the toe together. To blunt the toe, work half of the decreases (half of 56 = 28), which will leave 22 stitches for the instep and 22 for the heel (72–28 = 44). Then continue to decrease every round from that point until 16 total stitches remain.

Yoga Moves

Combine your favorite colors and a special message to create socks that reflect your personality and make you smile. This new twist on a traditional style is a great way to learn or practice two-color stranded Fair Isle techniques. Like yoga, these socks will help you remember to "relax" and "breathe."

Size	Woman's large/Man's medium *Option:* For a smaller sock (Woman's S–M), work the sock on a US #1.5 (2.5mm) or US #2 (2.75mm) needle, *or the size needed to obtain gauge* of 26 sts = 4" (10cm).
Yarn	Dalegarn Falk, 100% wool, sport weight, 1.75 oz (50g)/116 yd (106m) skeins 2 skeins mc (navy) #5563 1 skein cc1 (purple fuchsia) #5036 1 skein cc2 (mustard green) #9146 1 skein cc3 (azure turquoise) #6027
Needles	One 5-needle set US #2–2.5 (2.75–3mm) double-point needles, *or size you need to obtain correct gauge* **Hint:** You may use a larger needle for the stranded areas if your gauge in the stranded areas is tighter than your gauge in the solid color after the roll at the beginning of the sock.
Gauge	24 sts = 4" (10cm) in stockinette stitch
Other supplies	Tape measure, reinforcing yarn (optional), yarn needle, needle and stitch gauge
Abbreviations	**cc** = contrast color; **K** = knit; **K2tog** = knit 2 stitches together; **mc** = main color; **P** = purl; **P2tog** = purl 2 stitches together; **rs** = right side; **ssk** = slip, slip, knit the 2 slipped stitches together; **st(s)** = stitch(es); **ws** = wrong side

GETTING STARTED

Setup: Using cc1, loosely cast on 56 stitches.

Divide stitches evenly among 4 needles, 14 stitches on each needle. This sock begins and ends in the center back of the leg and heel, and center bottom of the sole.

Join into a round being careful not to twist stitches. (For instructions, see Joining: Trading Places and Getting Ready to Work, page 16.)

WORKING THE SOCK TOP

Note: You have a choice of variations for the sock top: double rolled or traditional ribbing. The rolled top can be worn "up" with reverse stockinette edge or rolled down to create two contrasting rolls.

Rolled Top only:
Round 1: Using cc1, purl every round for 1" (2.5cm).

Round 2: Change to mc and knit every round for 1" (2.5cm).

Ribbed Top only: Using cc1, K1, P1 to end of each round for 1½" (4cm), or desired length.

WORKING THE SOCK LEG

Using mc, knit to end of each round until sock measures 2" (5cm) from introduction of mc.

Note: Begin here to work Chart A (page 84), Rounds 1–37, changing colors as indicated. Work chart from right to left, beginning on Line 1 at bottom of chart; repeat 4-stitch pattern to end of each round. Note that the lettering is worked on Rounds 17–21, using the Alphabet Chart provided. Below, I walk you through the chart, round by round. For advice on starting new yarns, see Splicing Ends Together, page 123.

Round 1: Using cc1, knit to end of round.

Round 2: Using cc1 and mc, *K1 cc1, K1 mc; repeat from * to end of round.

Rounds 3–4: Using mc, knit to end of each round.

Round 5: Using cc2 and mc, *K1 cc2, K1 mc; repeat from * to end of round.

Rounds 6–7: Using mc, knit to end of each round.

Round 8: Using cc1 and mc, *K1 cc1, K1 mc; repeat from * to end of round.

Round 9: Using cc1, knit to end of round.

Rounds 10–11: Using mc, knit to end of each round.

Round 12: Using mc and cc3, K1 mc, *K1 cc3, K3 mc; repeat from * to last 3 sts, K1 cc3, K2 mc.

Round 13: Using cc3 and mc, *K1 cc3, K1 mc; repeat from * to end of round.

Round 14: Using mc and cc3, *K3 mc, K1 cc3; repeat from * to end of round.

Rounds 15–16: Using mc, knit to end of each round.

Rounds 17–21: Work the lettering on these rounds. Using the alphabet provided (page 84) and graph paper, center words of your choice and use mc as the background color to separate letters and words, and cc2 for the lettering. The graph will look upside down when you work it on a top-down sock, as shown in the Alphabet Chart (page 84) for use.

Rounds 22–23: Using mc, knit to end of each round.

Round 24: Using mc and cc3, *K3 mc, K1 cc3; repeat from * to end of round.

Round 25: Using cc3 and mc, *K1 cc3, K1 mc; repeat from * to end of round.

Round 26: Using mc and cc3, K1 mc, *K1 cc3, K3 mc; repeat from * to last 3 sts, K1 cc3, K2 mc.

Rounds 27–28: Using mc, knit to end of each round.

Round 29: Using cc1, knit to end of round.

Round 30: Using cc1 and mc, *K1 cc1, K1 mc; repeat from * to end of round.

Rounds 31–32: Using mc, knit to end of each round.

Round 33: Using cc2 and mc, *K1 cc2, K1 mc; repeat from * to end of round.

Rounds 34–35: Using mc, knit to end of each round.

Round 36: Using cc1 and mc, *K1 cc1, K1 mc; repeat from * to end of round.

Round 37: Using cc1, knit to end of round. *(Chart A completed.)*

Rounds 38–39: Using mc, knit to end of each round.

Sock length will be approximately 6¾" (16cm) from introduction of mc.

MAKING THE HEEL FLAP

Setup
Row 1 (rs): Using mc, K14 stitches from Needle 1 onto Needle 4 for the heel flap. You will work the 28 heel flap stitches back and forth using 2 needles. Break off mc, leaving a 6" (15cm) tail to weave in.

Row 2 (ws): Using cc2 and reinforcing yarn, if desired, turn to wrong side and purl to end of needle. Turn back to right side.

Note: In working the heel flap and turning the heel, slip stitches purlwise with yarn in front on wrong-side rows and yarn in back on right-side rows.

Row 1 (rs): *Slip 1, K1; repeat from * to end of needle. Turn.

Row 2 (ws): Slip 1, P to end of needle. Turn.

Rows 3–26: Repeat Rows 1 and 2, or work until the heel flap is approximately 2½" (6cm), or desired length.

Row 27: Repeat Row 1. Turn over to wrong side in preparation for turning the heel. Break off cc2, leaving a tail. Heel flap is complete.

TURNING THE HEEL

Setup: Attach cc1 and begin turning the heel.

Row 1: Slip 1, P14, P2tog, P1, turn, leaving 10 sts unworked.

Row 2: Slip 1, K3, ssk, K1, turn, leaving 10 sts unworked.

Row 3: Slip 1, P4, P2tog, P1, leaving 8 sts unworked.

Row 4: Slip 1, K5, ssk, K1, leaving 8 sts unworked.

Row 5: Slip 1, P6, P2tog, P1, leaving 6 sts unworked.

Row 6: Slip 1, K7, ssk, K1, leaving 6 sts unworked.

Row 7: Slip 1, P8, P2tog, P1, leaving 4 sts unworked.

Row 8: Slip 1, K9, ssk, K1, leaving 4 sts unworked.

Row 9: Slip 1, P10, P2tog, P1, leaving 2 sts unworked.

Row 10: Slip 1, K11, ssk, K1, leaving 2 sts unworked.

Row 11: Slip 1, P12, P2tog, P1, leaving 0 sts unworked.

Row 12: Slip 1, K13, ssk, K1, leaving 0 sts unworked.

You now have 16 heel stitches. Break off cc1, leaving a tail for weaving in.

PICKING UP STITCHES FOR HEEL GUSSET

Note: For techniques, see Secrets for Tight, Smooth Gussets, pages 26–29.

Setup

Attach mc. With the heel stitch needle, pick up and knit 14 stitches along the right side of the heel flap. This is Needle 1.

Needle 2: Knit 14 stitches.

Needle 3: Knit 14 stitches.

Using an empty needle, pick up and knit 14 stitches along the left side of the heel flap. Then knit 8 of the remaining heel stitches onto same needle. This is Needle 4. This is the center back, beginning and end of rounds.

You now have

Needle 1: 22 stitches

Needle 2: 14 stitches

Needle 3: 14 stitches

Needle 4: 22 stitches

Total on all 4 needles: 72 stitches

WORKING THE GUSSET DECREASES

Round 1

Needle 1: Knit to last 3 sts, K2tog, K1.

Needles 2 and 3: Knit to end of each needle.

Needle 4: K1, ssk, K to end of needle.

Round 2: Knit all stitches.

Rounds 3–16: Repeat Rounds 1 and 2. You now have a total of 56 stitches (14 stitches on each needle.) Make no further decreases.

Rounds 17–24: Continuing to use mc, knit to end of each round, or work until measurement from the completion of the gusset decreases is about 1" (2.5cm).

Note: For a shorter foot, you may want to stop in preparation for the foot colorwork after knitting only ¾" (2cm) after the gusset.

WORKING THE PATTERNED SOCK FOOT

NOTE: Work Chart B (page 84), Lines 1–17, changing colors as indicated. Work the chart from right to left, beginning on Line 1 at the bottom, and repeat the 4-stitch pattern to the end of each round. The text below corresponds to the chart on page 84.

Round 1: Using cc1, knit to end of round.

Round 2: Using cc1 and mc,* K1 cc1, K1 mc; repeat from * to end of round.

Rounds 3–4: Using mc, knit to end of each round.

Round 5: Using cc2 and mc, *K1 cc2, K1 mc; repeat from * to end of round.

Rounds 6–7: Using mc, knit to end of each round.

Round 8: Using mc and cc3, K1 mc, *K1 cc3, K3 mc; repeat from * to last 2 sts, K2 mc.

Round 9: Using cc3 and mc, *K1 cc3, K1 mc; repeat from * to end of round.

Round 10: Using mc and cc3, *K3 mc, K1 cc3; repeat from * to end of round.

Rounds 11–12: Using mc, knit to end of each round.

Round 13: Using cc2 and mc, *K1 cc2, K1 mc; repeat from * to end of round.

Rounds 14–15: Using mc, knit to end of each round.

Round 16: Using cc1 and mc, *K1 cc1, K1 mc; repeat from * to end of round.

Round 17: Using cc1, knit to end of round. (*Chart B is complete.*)

Next Rounds: Using mc, knit to end of each round for 1½" (4cm), or until measurement from back of heel is about 8" (20cm), or desired length. Break off mc, leaving 6" (15cm) tail to weave in.

You now have 56 stitches.

SHAPING THE ROUND TOE

Round 1: Using cc3, *K5, K2tog; repeat from * to end of round. You now have 12 stitches on each needle, and a total of 48 stitches.

Rounds 2–4: Knit to end of each round.

Round 5: *K4, K2tog; repeat from * to end of round. You now have 10 stitches on each needle, and a total of 40 stitches.

Rounds 6–8: Knit to end of each round.

Round 9: *K3, K2tog; repeat from * to end of round. You now have 8 stitches on each needle, and a total of 32 stitches.

Rounds 10–11: Knit to end of each round.

Round 12: *K2, K2tog; repeat from * to end of round. You now have 6 stitches on each needle, and a total of 24 stitches.

Rounds 13–14: Knit to end of each round.

Round 15: *K1, K2tog; repeat from * to end of round. You now have 4 stitches on each needle, and a total of 16 stitches.

Rounds 16–17: Knit to end of each round.

CLOSING THE TOE AND FINISHING THE SOCK

Round 18: K2tog to end of round. You now have 2 stitches on each needle, and a total of 8 stitches.

Break off yarn, leaving a 6" (15cm) tail. Pull tail through remaining stitches with a yarn needle. Cinch stitches up firmly to close toe. Take yarn through to wrong side and weave in end. Weave in any other loose ends.

Lightly block with spray mist or steam to smooth out color pattern work and the rest of the sock. Pat gently into shape.

No More "Ladders"

When knitting in the round, strive for an even-textured fabric. Try to avoid making a "ladder" – that line of loose stitches that makes the place where you changed from one needle to the next apparent, rather than invisible, as it should be. Here are some tips that may help:

- Knit the first few stitches on each new needle tighter than usual and give each of those stitches a little tug before moving on to the next one.
- Knit with five, rather than four, if using double-point needles.
- Lay the needle tip forming the new stitch up against the last stitch and knit it with adequate tension to prevent any slack.

Alphabet Chart

NOTE: Letters are worked upside down as presented on chart, but will appear right side up on the completed top-down sock.

Chart A

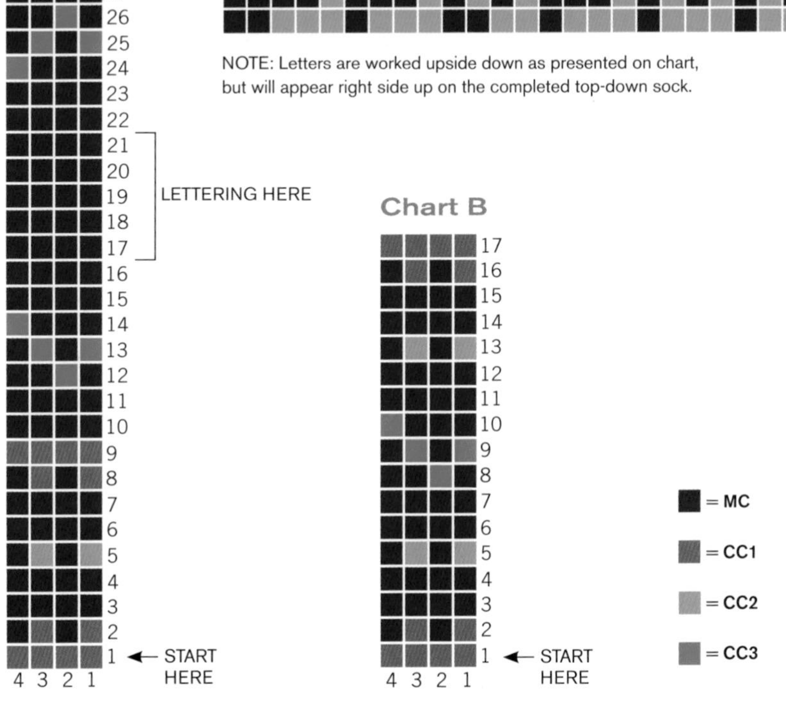

Sizing the Sock for Good Fit

Three dimensions need to be considered in deciding what size to make your socks:

1. Width of foot or leg (relates to size shown in patterns)
2. Length of foot
3. Length of heel flap

Using the chart below, sock length can be estimated from the wearer's shoe size. To calculate stitches for a specific foot width, multiply gauge (the number of stitches per inch) by the number of inches needed to go around the widest part of the foot. Reduce those stitches by 10–15 percent for "stretch" and round up or down to the nearest number divisible by 4 or your pattern multiple.

To determine heel flap length, measure from ankle bone to foot sole. Making the flap too long produces a baggy foot; making it too short makes the instep and foot feel too tight. The length of the average heel flap for a woman is 2½" (6.4cm) and 2¾" (7cm) for the average man.

Socks stretch, enabling a sock to fit different foot sizes quite comfortably. Ribbed socks have more stretch and are a good choice to make for people not available to be measured. To gauge sock fit, insert your hand (or very carefully your foot) into the sock after working several inches. The way your hand fits into the sock is usually a good indicator of how it will fit on you or someone else with your foot width.

Adult Sock Length Guidelines

	US		EUR	
	SHOE SIZE	LENGTH	SHOE SIZE	LENGTH
Woman's	6–8	9"–9⅝"	36–38	23–24.5cm
	9–10½	10"–10½"	39–41	25.5–26.5cm
	11–14	10⅝"–11½"	42–45	27–30cm
Man's	5–7	9"–9½"	36.5–38.5	23–24.5cm
	8–11	10"–11"	39.5–45	25.5–28cm
	12–15	11¼"–12¼"	46–49	28.5–31cm

Best Foot Forward

These classic unisex socks highlight the beauty of both luxury and traditional yarns. The flattering lines of vertical rib ensure a snug fit, for socks that feel as good as they look. You can knit them in fingering- or worsted-weight yarns. Either version will let you put your best foot forward!

Size	Woman's large/Man's medium
Yarn	**Fingering-Weight Version (shown at right)** Naturally NZ Yarns Waikiwi, 55% NZ merino/20% nylon/ 15% alpaca/10% possum, machine washable, 1.75 oz (50g)/ 198 yd (181m) skeins 2 skeins Toast #401 (3 skeins may be needed for the Man's medium size) NOTE: This yarn from New Zealand is a heavy fingering weight that can be used either as a fingering- or sport-weight yarn. Just be sure to swatch to achieve the proper gauge for the socks you are making (see Getting the Right Gauge, pages 12–13). **Worsted-Weight Version (shown on page 94)** Cascade 220, 100% wool, 3.5 oz (100g)/220 yd (202m) skeins 2 skeins (Natural/#8010)
Needles	**Fingering-Weight Version:** One 4-needle set US #1.5 (2.5mm) double-point needles, *or size you need to obtain correct gauge* **Worsted-Weight Version:** One 4-needle set US #3 (3.25mm) double-point needles, *or size you need to obtain correct gauge*
Gauge	**Fingering-Weight Version:** 28 sts = 4" (10cm) in stockinette stitch **Worsted-Weight Version:** 24 sts = 4" (10cm) in stockinette stitch
Other supplies	Tape measure, yarn needle, needle and stitch gauge
Abbreviations	**K** = knit; **K2tog** = knit 2 stitches together; **P** = purl; **P2tog** = purl 2 stitches together; **rs** = right side; **rnd(s)** = rounds; **sl** = slip; **ssk** = slip, slip, knit the 2 slipped stitches together; **st(s)** = stitches; **TW** = Twist right = K2tog leaving both sts on left needle, K again into front of first st on left needle and slip both sts off needle; **ws** = wrong side; **wyb** = with yarn in back; **wyf** = with yarn in front

GETTING STARTED	FINGERING WT	WORSTED WT
Note: This pattern is worked on three needles instead of four. To adapt this pattern to use four needles, divide the instep stitches on Needle 1 between two needles. Rounds start and end on the right side of the sock as worn. You may adjust the suggested lengths for ribbing, leg, and foot by working more or fewer rounds, as desired.		
Setup: Loosely cast on	70 sts	56 sts
Divide stitches among 3 needles as follows:		
Needle 1 (instep):	36 sts	29 sts
Needle 2 (heel):	18 sts	13 sts
Needle 3 (heel):	16 sts	14 sts
Join into a round, being careful not to twist stitches. (For instructions, see Joining: Trading Places and Getting Ready to Work, page 16.)		
WORKING THE RIBBING AND SOCK LEG		
Work K1, P1 (ribbing) for	12 rnds	8 rnds
Ribbing will measure approximately	1¼" (3cm)	1" (2.5cm)
Next Round: Purl to end of round.		
Next Round: Knit to end of round.		
Note: Round 1 below, in both fingering and worsted weights, sets up the Cable Twist Rib Pattern Stitch (below) for leg and instep of foot down to toe shaping.		

Cable Twist Rib Pattern Stitch
(multiple of 7)

Round 1: *K1, P2, TW, P2; repeat from * to end of round.
Rounds 2–4: *K1, P2, K2, P2; repeat from * to end of round.

	FINGERING WT	WORSTED WT
Fingering Weight only: **Round 1** (Setup) Needle 1 (instep): *K1, P2, TW, P2; repeat from * to last st, K1. You now have	36 sts	
Needle 2: *P2, TW, P2, K1; repeat from * to last 4 sts, P2, TW. You now have	18 sts	
Needle 3: P2, *K1, P2, TW, P2; repeat from * to end of needle. You now have	16 sts	
You have a total of	70 sts	
Rounds 2–4 Needle 1: *K1, P2, K2, P2; repeat from * to last st, K1. You now have	36 sts	
Needle 2: *P2, K2, P2, K1; repeat from* to last 4 sts, P2, K2. You now have	18 sts	
Needle 3: P2, *K1, P2, K2, P2; repeat from * to end of needle. You now have	16 sts	
You have a total of	70 sts	
Worsted Weight only: **Round 1** (Setup) Needle 1 (instep): *K1, P2, TW, P2; repeat from * to last st, K1. You now have		29 sts
Needle 2: P2, TW, P2, K1, P2, TW, P2. You now have		13 sts
Needle 3: *K1, P2, TW, P2; repeat from * to end of needle. You now have		14 sts
You have a total of		56 sts
Rounds 2–4 Needle 1: *K1, P2, K2, P2; repeat from * to last st, K1. You now have		29 sts
Needle 2: P2, K2, P2, K1, P2, K2, P2. You now have		13 sts
Needle 3: *K1, P2, K2, P2; repeat from * to end of needle. You now have		14 sts
You have a total of		56 sts
Both Weights: **Next Rounds:** Repeat Rounds 1–4	14 more times	11 more times
Measurement from cast-on edge will be approximately 7½" (19cm). End having just worked Round 1.		

MAKING THE HEEL FLAP	FINGERING WT	WORSTED WT
Note: Divide the instep stitches onto 2 needles, move heel stitches onto one needle. Needles 1 and 2 now hold the instep stitches. Needle 3 holds the heel stitches. While you work the heel flap, the instep stitches wait on 2 needles until needed again. You will be working on the heel flap back and forth in rows on 2 needles/tips. You now have		
Needles 1 and 2 (instep):	36 sts	29 sts
Needles 3 (heel):	34 sts	27 sts
While working the heel flap, slip all slipped sts purlwise, wyf for ws rows and wyb for rs rows.		
Setup: Turn last needle worked (Needle 3) over to wrong side. Slip the stitches from Needle 2 to Needle 3. You now have	34 sts	27 sts
Row 1 (ws): Slip 1, purl to end of row.		
Row 2 (rs): *Slip 1, K1; repeat from * to end of row. (*Worsted Weight only:* End K2.)		
Repeat Rows 1 and 2	17 more times	13 more times
When the heel measures 2½" (6cm), end with Row 2.		
TURNING THE HEEL		
Turn over to wrong side to begin.		
Fingering weight only: **Row 1 (ws):** Sl1, P18, P2tog, P1, turn, leaving ____ unworked.	12 sts	
Row 2 (rs): Sl1, K5, ssk, K1, turn, leaving ____ unworked.	12 sts	
Row 3: Sl1, P6, P2tog, P1, turn, leaving ____ unworked.	10 sts	
Row 4: Sl1, K7, ssk, K1, turn, leaving ____ unworked.	10 sts	
Row 5: Sl1, P8, P2tog, P1, turn, leaving ____ unworked.	8 sts	
Row 6: Sl1, K9, ssk, K1, turn, leaving ____ unworked.	8 sts	

	FINGERING WT	WORSTED WT
Row 7: Sl1, P10, P2tog, P1, turn, leaving ____ unworked.	6 sts	
Row 8: Sl1, K11, ssk, K1, turn, leaving ____ unworked.	6 sts	
Row 9: Sl1, P12, P2tog, P1, turn, leaving ____ unworked.	4 sts	
Row 10: Sl1, K13, ssk, K1, turn, leaving ____ unworked.	4 sts	
Row 11: Sl1, P14, P2tog, P1, turn, leaving ____ unworked.	2 sts	
Row 12: Sl1, K15, ssk, K1, turn, leaving ____ unworked.	2 sts	
Row 13: Sl1, P16, P2tog, P1, turn, leaving ____ unworked.	0 sts	
Row 14: Sl1, K17, ssk, K1.		
Fingering-weight only: Heel turning complete. You now have	20 sts	
Worsted Weight only: **Row 1:** Sl1, P15, P2tog, P1, turn, leaving ____ unworked.		8 sts
Row 2: Sl1, K6, ssk, K1, turn, leaving ____ unworked.		8 sts
Row 3: Sl1, P7, P2tog, P1, turn, leaving ____ unworked.		6 sts
Row 4: Sl1, K8, ssk, K1, turn, leaving ____ unworked.		6 sts
Row 5: Sl1, P9, P2tog, P1, turn, leaving ____ unworked.		4 sts
Row 6: Sl1, K10, ssk, K1, turn, leaving ____ unworked.		4 sts
Row 7: Sl1, P11, P2tog, P1, turn, leaving ____ unworked.		2 sts
Row 8: Sl1, K12, ssk, K1, turn, leaving ____ unworked.		2 sts
Row 9: Sl1, P13, P2tog, P1, turn, leaving ____ unworked.		0 sts
Row 10: Sl1, K14, ssk, K1, turn, leaving ____ unworked.		0 sts
Worsted-weight only: Heel turning complete. You now have		17 sts

PICKING UP STITCHES FOR HEEL GUSSET	FINGERING WT	WORSTED WT
Note: For techniques, see Secrets for Tight, Smooth Gussets, pages 26–29.		
Setup	19 sts	14 sts
For Needle 3, using needle with remaining heel stitches, pick up and knit ___ along right side of heel flap.		
Slip instep stitches back onto one needle. Work Cable	36	29
Twist Rib Pattern Stitch Round 2 across the ___ instep stitches onto Needle 1.	19 sts	14 sts
With empty needle, pick up and knit ___ along left side of heel flap.	10 sts	8 sts
Onto same needle (Needle 2), knit ___ from Needle 3.		
Knit to end of Needle 3 to end round.		
You now have	36 sts	29 sts
Needle 1:	29 sts	22 sts
Needle 2:	29 sts	23 sts
Needle 3:	94 sts	74 sts
Total on all 3 needles:		

WORKING GUSSET DECREASES		
Note: The purl stitches at the beginning of Needle 2 and end of Needle 3 are intentional.		
Round 1		
Needle 1: Work Cable Twist Rib Pattern Stitch Round 3 to end of needle.		
Needle 2: P1, ssk, K to end of needle.		
Needle 3: Knit to last 3 sts, K2tog, P1.		
You now have	92 sts	72 sts
Round 2		
Needle 1: Work Cable Twist Rib Pattern Stitch Round 4 to end of needle.		
Needles 2 and 3: P1, K to last st on Needle 3, P1.		
Round 3		
Needle 1: Work Cable Twist Rib Pattern Stitch Round 1 to end of needle.		
Needle 2: P1, ssk, K to end of needle.		
Needle 3: Knit to last 3 sts, K2tog, P1.		
You now have	90 sts	70 sts

	FINGERING WT	WORSTED WT
Round 4 Needle 1: Work Cable Twist Rib Pattern Stitch Round 2 to end of needle. Needles 2 and 3: P1, K to last st on Needle 3, P1.		
Repeat Rounds 1–4 above until you have	70 sts	56 sts
WORKING THE SOCK FOOT		
Continue working the four pattern rounds established in Working Gusset Decreases, *but without working further decreases*, until 1½" (4cm) from desired length of foot. **NOTE:** Be sure to work the correct pattern round following the last one worked for gusset decreases above. That is, if gusset decreases ended with Round 3, start sock foot by working Round 4.		
Round 1 Needle 1: Work Cable Twist Rib Pattern Stitch Round 1 to end of needle. Needles 2 and 3: Knit to end of each needle.		
Rounds 2–4 Needle 1: Work Cable Twist Rib Pattern Stitch Rounds 2, 3, or 4 to end of needle. Needles 2 and 3: Knit to end of each needle.		
Next Round: When foot is desired length to toe shaping, transfer 1 stitch from Needle 1 to Needle 2, while working Round 2, 3, or 4, whichever is appropriate to maintain pattern. For example: Needle 1: Work pattern as established to last stitch, slip that stitch onto Needle 2. Needles 2 and 3: Knit to end of each needle to complete round. You now have		
Needle 1:	35 sts	28 sts
Needle 2:	18 sts	14 sts
Needle 3:	17 sts	14 sts
Total on all 3 needles:	70 sts	56 sts

SHAPING THE TOE	FINGERING WT	WORSTED WT
Round 1 Needle 1: K1, ssk, K to last 3 sts, K2tog, K1. Needle 2: K1, ssk, K to end of needle. Needle 3: Knit to last 3 sts, K2tog, K1.		
Round 2: Knit to end of each needle.		
Next Rounds: Repeat Rounds 1 and 2 until you have	42 sts	36 sts
Next Rounds: Repeat Round 1 (decrease round) every round until you have	14 sts	12 sts
CLOSING THE TOE AND FINISHING THE SOCK		
SETUP: Slip the Needle 2 and 3 stitches onto one needle, and hold them parallel to the Needle 1 stitches.		
Graft front and back stitches together using Kitchener stitch. (For instructions, see pages 29–30.)		
Weave in any loose ends.		
To block, lightly mist or steam sock and pat into shape.		

Be Your Own Designer

Here's one way to proceed in personalizing or modifying a pattern after getting comfortable with sock knitting:

- Select a pattern that appeals to you. See Barbara G. Walker's four-volume, *Treasury of Knitting Patterns* and other stitch dictionaries, as well as patterns in magazines, books, and catalogs. Open yourself to possibilities!
- Make a gauge swatch (in the round) with yarn you like and think might work.
- Check the fabric density of your swatch, changing needle size until you get the right "feel."
- Measure gauge and calculate stitches required to produce the desired sock size. Note that slip stitch, cable, and twisted stitch patterns pull in, making it necessary to add more stitches than for stockinette stitch. Lace patterns, in contrast, tend to be more open and to stretch out more than stockinette stitch, resulting in a need for fewer stitches. Yarn overs produce more stretch or "give," an important consideration when planning lace. It is a good idea to block your swatch using any new stitch to see what it will be like in a sock after blocking and washing. Treat it like a finished sock, blocking and drying it before measuring the gauge.
- Consider breaking "rules," such as variegated yarns not being suitable for cables or certain patterns. Play with patterns, making various swatches until you hit on something pleasing to you. Try something different, like combining a number of different ribs, one after the other, in a "traditional" ribbed-style sock. Think about putting words in surprising places, in surprising colors! Make a cuff with a color or texture pattern you want to try out and follow that with interesting ribs down the leg. Play and have fun creating your own special socks!

You've Got Rhythm

This trio of patterns has variety and something for everyone. Rhythm is worked in brightly colored hand-painted yarn using a rhythmic, slip-stitch pattern. A two-color version – Double Time – provides double the fun, while a shimmering rib dances down the third sock in Shimmy Rib. All three socks use the same easy lace cuff. Or, work a traditional knit-and-purl ribbing, for a stretchy, unisex pattern you're sure to return to again and again.

Sizes	Woman's medium–large (size adjustable, see Note below)
Yarn	**Shimmy Rib (shown at right):** Lorna's Laces Shepherd Sock Yarn, 80% superwash wool/20% nylon, fingering weight, 1.75 oz (50g)/ 215 yd (197m) skeins: 2 skeins Berry #23ns **Rhythm (shown on page 103, top):** Misti Alpaca Hand Paint, 50% alpaca/30% merino wool/10% silk/10% nylon, fingering weight, 3.5 oz (100g)/437 yd (400m) skeins: 1 skein Manu #18 **Double Time (shown on page 103, bottom):** Crystal Palace Panda Silk, 52% bamboo/43% superwash merino wool/5% combed silk, fingering weight, 1.75 oz (50g)/ 204 yd (188m) skeins: 2 skeins mc (Lilac Mist #3020), 2 skeins cc (Treasure Chest #5109)
Needles	US #1 (2.25mm), *or size you need to obtain correct gauge:* set of 4 or 5 double-point needles, one 32"–40" *OR* two 24" circular needles
Gauge	34 stitches = 4" (10cm) in stockinette stitch **Note:** Sizing up or down in needle size to increase or decrease the circumference of these socks works well to adjust size. This can be done for the entire sock or just the cuff to increase the circumference of the sock top.
Other supplies	Tape measure, yarn needle, yarn and needle gauge
Abbreviations	**cc** = contrast color; **K** = knit; **K2tog** = knit 2 stitches together; **mc** = main color; **P** = purl; **P2tog** = purl 2 stitches together; **rs** = right side; **ssk** = slip, slip, knit the 2 slipped stitches together; **st(s)** = stitch(es); **ws** = wrong side; **YO** = yarn over

GETTING STARTED

Note: In all 3 patterns, the first half of the stitches cast on and worked become the instep stitches and the remaining (last half) are the heel stitches.

Setup: Loosely cast on 72 stitches. Divide stitches evenly among the needles. Join into a round, being careful not to twist. (For instructions, see Joining: Trading Places and Getting Ready to Work, page 16.)

WORKING THE CUFF

Round 1: Purl to end of each needle.

Round 2: Knit to end of each needle.

Round 3: *P1, ssk, K1, YO, K1, YO, K1, K2tog, P1; repeat from * to end of round.

Round 4: P1, K7, *P2, K7; repeat from * to last stitch, P1.

Rounds 5–8: Repeat Rounds 3 and 4 two more times.

Rounds 9–10: Purl to end of each needle.

Rounds 11–13: Knit to end of each needle.

Round 14: Purl to end of each needle.

Round 15: *P1, K2tog, K1, YO, K1, YO, K1, ssk, P1; repeat from * to end of round.

Round 16: Purl to end of each needle.

Rounds 17–19: Knit to end of each needle.

Rounds 20–21: Purl to end of each needle.

Working with Color

- When changing yarn colors, bring the new color up from under the old to prevent holes.
- One of the Double Time sock models shows the cc and mc are reversed in both leg and foot sections. You may want to make your own changes.

Pattern Stitches (see charts, page 102)

Rhythm (multiple of 6 stitches)

Rounds 1 and 2: Knit to end of each needle.

Round 3: K1, *slip 1, K2; repeat from * ending with slip 1, K1.

Round 4: P1, *slip 1, P2; repeat from * ending with slip 1, P1.

Double Time (multiple of 6 stitches)

Rounds 1 and 2: Using mc, knit to end of each needle.

Round 3: Using cc, K1, *slip 1, K2; repeat from * to last stitch, K1.

Round 4: Using cc, P1, *slip 1, P2; repeat from * to last stitch, P1.

Shimmy Rib (multiple of 6 stitches)

Rounds 1–4: *P1, K4, P1; repeat from * to end of round

Rounds 5–8: *K2, P2, K2; repeat from * to end of round

WORKING THE SOCK LEG

Work your chosen stitch pattern until the leg measures approximately 7" (or desired length) from cast on, slipping all stitches as if to purl, holding yarn in back.

Rhythm and Double Time only: End with Round 2 of the pattern. Turn work.

Shimmy Rib only: End with either Round 4 or Round 8. Turn work.

MAKING THE HEEL FLAP

Note: Beginning on the wrong side, work the heel flap back and forth on 36 heel stitches while the instep stitches wait on their needle(s) until you use them again for Picking Up Stitches for the Heel Gusset (page 101). Slip all heel stitches purlwise, with yarn in front on the wrong side and with yarn in back on right-side rows.

Double Time only: Begin working heel using mc.

Row 1 (ws): Slip 1, P to end of heel stitches, turn.

Row 2 (rs): *Slip 1, K1; repeat from * to end of heel stitches.

Repeat Rows 1 and 2 until heel flap is approx. 2½" (6cm) long or desired length, ending with a right-side row. (Nineteen repeats of Rows 1 and 2 = 2½" (6cm) in pattern models.)

TURNING THE HEEL

Row 1 (ws): Slip 1, P20, P2tog, P1, turn, leaving 12 stitches unworked.

Row 2 (rs): Slip 1, K7, ssk, K1, turn, leaving 12 stitches unworked.

Row 3: Slip 1, P8, P2tog, P1, turn, leaving 10 stitches unworked.

Row 4: Slip 1, K9, ssk, K1, turn, leaving 10 stitches unworked.

Row 5: Slip 1, P10, P2tog, P1, turn, leaving 8 stitches unworked.

Row 6: Slip 1, K11, ssk, K1, turn, leaving 8 stitches unworked.

Row 7: Slip 1, P12, P2tog, P1, turn, leaving 6 stitches unworked.

Row 8: Slip 1, K13, ssk, K1, turn, leaving 6 stitches unworked.

Row 9: Slip 1, P14, P2tog, P1, turn, leaving 4 stitches unworked.

Row 10: Slip 1, K15, ssk, K1, turn, leaving 4 stitches unworked.

Row 11: Slip 1, P16, P2tog, P1, turn, leaving 2 stitches unworked.

Row 12: Slip 1, K17, ssk, K1, turn, leaving 2 stitches unworked.

Row 13: Slip 1, P18, P2tog, P1, turn, leaving 0 stitches unworked.

Row 14: Slip 1, K19, ssk, K1. Heel turning is complete. You now have 22 stitches. End having just worked a right-side row.

Optional Narrower Heel

You may want to try this approach for turning the heel instead.
Row 1: Slip 1, P18, P2tog, P1, turn, leaving 14 unworked.
Row 2: Slip 1, K3, ssk, K1, turn, leaving 14 unworked.
Row 3: Slip 1, P4, P2tog, P1, turn, leaving 12 unworked.
Row 4: Slip 1, K5, ssk, K1, turn, leaving 12 unworked.
Row 5: Slip 1, P6, P2tog, P1, turn, leaving 10 unworked.
Row 6: Slip 1, K7, ssk, K1, turn, leaving 10 unworked.
Continue from Row 3 instructions above, except you will be leaving 2 stitches less each time (for example, you will be leaving 8 stitches instead of 10 stitches.)
After heel turning, 20 stitches will remain. End with a right-side row.

PICKING UP STITCHES FOR HEEL GUSSET

Note: For techniques, see Secrets for Tight, Smooth Gussets, pages 26–29. Pick up enough stitches to avoid holes or looseness along the edge of heel flap, even if this means that you pick up slightly more or less than 19.

Setup: Using the appropriate needle, pick up and knit 19 stitches up the right side of heel flap. Then work across all instep stitches, beginning with the next row of the pattern you have chosen.

Rhythm and Double Time only: Work Round 3.

Shimmy Rib only: Work either Round 5 or 1, depending on whether you ended with Round 4 or Round 8.

Pick up and knit 19 stitches along the left side of the heel flap.

Continue to knit across the remaining heel stitches (the 22 stitches remaining after heel turning plus the 19 picked up along the right side of the flap or the 20 stitches remaining for the narrow heel turning option).

WORKING GUSSET DECREASES

Rhythm and Double Time only: Begin instep by working pattern Row 4.

Shimmy Rib only: Begin the instep by working either pattern Row 6 or 2, depending on whether the last pattern row worked before the heel was Row 5 or Row 1.

Round 1

Instep stitches: Work in pattern as established.

Heel stitches: K1, ssk, K to last 3 heel stitches, K2tog, K1. (You have decreased 2 stitches.)

Round 2

Instep stitches: Work in pattern as established.

Heel stitches: Knit to end of each needle.

Next Rounds: Repeat Rounds 1 and 2 until you have a total of 72 stitches (36 for instep and 36 for heel).

Rhythm and Double Time only: End by working pattern Row 2 or 4.

WORKING THE SOCK FOOT

Note: To fit various lengths, make the sock longer or shorter by working more or fewer rounds for the foot.

Double Time only: Continue slip-stitch pattern in mc for one pattern repeat (4 rounds) beyond the last gusset decrease. Then reverse mc and cc, working Rows 1 and 2 in cc and 3 and 4 in mc until 2" (5cm) from the desired length of the sock foot or 1½" (4cm) if using a rounder toe (see Making a More Blunt, Rounded Toe, page 75).

Continue working without making further decreases, patterning instep stitches and knitting sole stitches as established. Measuring from the back of the heel, work until the foot is 2" from the desired length of the sock foot.

Rhythm and Double Time only: End with pattern Row 2 or 4.

SHAPING THE TOE

Note: The toes of each pattern stitch are shaped in the same manner using stockinette stitch (knitting every round).

Round 1: Knit to end of each needle.

Round 2

Instep stitches: K1, ssk, K to last 3 instep stitches, K2tog, K1.

Sole stitches: K1, ssk, K to last 3 heel stitches, K2tog, K1.

Round 3: Knit to end of each needle.

Next Rounds: Repeat Rounds 2 and 3 until 16 stitches remain (8 instep and 8 sole stitches).

CLOSING THE TOE AND FINISHING THE SOCK

Break yarn, leaving a 10" (25cm) tail. Hold the remaining stitches parallel on two needles or needle tips. Using the tail threaded on a yarn needle, graft the front and back stitches together using Kitchener stitch (see pages 29–30). Weave in the end after grafting the toe. Weave in any other loose ends.

To block, lightly mist or steam the sock and pat it gently into shape.

Rhythm

6	5	4	3	2	1	
•	V	•	•	V	•	4
	V			V		3
						2
						1

Double Time

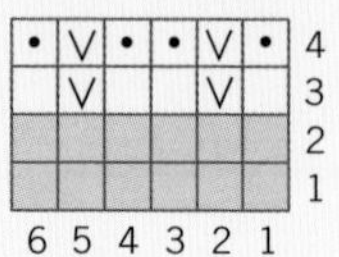

Shimmy Rib

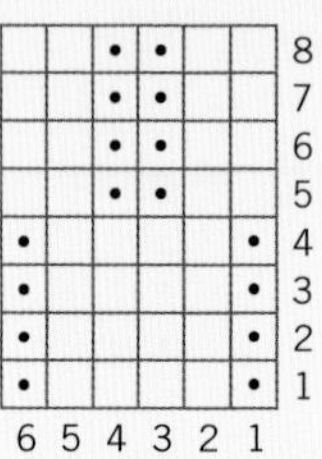

- **MC** MAIN COLOR
- **CC** CONTRAST COLOR
- **K** KNIT
- • **P** PURL
- V **SL** SLIP slip stitch as if to purl, holding yarn in back

Off the Cuff

Sensible socks can be attractive! These classic, cuffed anklets with contrasting trim and toes are ready for anything. Use a soft cotton-blend yarn to make them an instant and comfy favorite. Instructions include two sizes and can be adjusted for more. Begin with a small band of stockinette stitch that curls under to create an interesting cuff edging. Add more stripes where you want to personalize your socks.

Sizes	Woman's small–medium Woman's large/Man's medium
Yarn	Lana Grossa Meilenweit Cotton, 45% cotton/42% wool/13% polyamid, fingering weight, 1.75 oz (50g)/208 yd (190m) skeins 2 skeins mc Lt. Olive/#26 1 skein cc Natural/#24 **Note:** 1 pair Woman's small–medium takes approximately 360 yards mc and 70 yards cc.
Needles	One 5-needle set US #1 (2.25mm) double-point needles, *or size you need to obtain correct gauge*
Gauge	32 sts = 4" (10cm) in stockinette stitch
Other supplies	Tape measure, yarn needle, yarn and needle gauge
Abbreviations	**cc** = contrast color; **K** = knit; **K2tog** = knit 2 stitches together; **mc** = main color; **P** = purl; **P2tog** = purl 2 stitches together; **rs** = right side; **ssk** = slip, slip, knit the 2 slipped stitches together; **st(s)** = stitch(es); **ws** = wrong side; **wyb** = with yarn in back; **wyf** = with yarn in front

Substitutions

This is the perfect pattern to adapt for a plain stockinette-stitch sock in fingering-weight yarn using either 64 stitches or 72 stitches. Substitute K1, P1 ribbing for the 1"–1½" (2.5–3.75cm) cuff instructions on page 106. Then knit all rounds to heel flap (7"/17.5cm) from cast on or desired length.

GETTING STARTED	WOMAN'S S–M	WOMAN'S L/ MAN'S M
Setup: Using cc, loosely cast on	64 sts	72 sts
Divide stitches evenly among 4 needles. On each needle you will have	16 sts	18 sts
Join into a round, being careful not to twist stitches. (For instructions, see Joining: Trading Places and Getting Ready to Work, page 16.) Rounds begin and end on the right side of the sock foot as worn.		
MAKING THE TRIMMED CUFF		
Contrasting Anklet Roll Edge: Continuing to use cc, knit to end of each round for ¾" (2cm). Break off cc, leaving a 6" (15cm) tail to weave in.		
Reverse Stockinette Stitch: Using mc, purl to end of each round for 1½" (4cm).		
Cuff Fold: Knit 1 round to create crease for folding cuff over.		
Next Rounds: K1, P1 (ribbing) to the end of each round until measurement from cuff fold is 1¾" (4.5cm). This will be about 20 rounds. Then knit all rounds for the next 2" (5cm) or desired length. This will be about 23 rounds.		
MAKING THE HEEL FLAP		
Note: You will work the heel stitches back and forth on two needles. In this section, slip all stitches purlwise when making the heel, wyf on wrong side and wyb on right-side rows. Work more or fewer rows for a longer or shorter heel flap. The instep stitches, which are on Needles 1 and 2, will wait while you work the heel flap. For the instep, there are	32 sts	36 sts
Setup: Slip the Needle 3 stitches onto Needle 4. Turn last needle used (Needle 4) around to wrong side to begin. The heel contains	32 sts	36 sts
Row 1 (ws): Slip 1, P to end of needle, turn to rs.		
Row 2 (rs): *Slip 1, K1; repeat from * across row, turn to ws.		

	WOMAN'S S–M	WOMAN'S L/ MAN'S M
Repeat Rows 1 and 2	17 more times	19 more times
The heel flap will measure	2¼" (6cm)	2¾" (7cm)
Last row worked is a right-side row.		
TURNING THE HEEL		
Note: Beginning on ws, turn the heel as follows, slipping all stitches purlwise wyf on ws rows and wyb on rs rows.		
Row 1 (ws): Slip 1, ___, P2tog, P1, turn, leaving ____ unworked.	P18 10 sts	P20 12 sts
Row 2: Slip 1, K7, ssk, K1, turn back to ws, leaving ____ unworked.	10 sts	12 sts
Row 3: Slip 1, P8, P2tog, P1, turn, leaving ____ unworked.	8 sts	10 sts
Row 4: Slip 1, K9, ssk, K1, turn, leaving ____ unworked.	8 sts	10 sts
Row 5: Slip 1, P10, P2tog, P1, turn, leaving ____ unworked.	6 sts	8 sts
Row 6: Slip 1, K11, ssk, K1, turn, leaving ____ unworked.	6 sts	8 sts
Row 7: Slip 1, P12, P2tog, P1, turn, leaving ____ unworked.	4 sts	6 sts
Row 8: Slip 1, K13, ssk, K1, turn, leaving ____ unworked.	4 sts	6 sts
Row 9: Slip 1, P14, P2tog, P1, turn, leaving ____ unworked.	2 sts	4 sts
Row 10: Slip 1, K15, ssk, K1, turn, leaving ____ unworked.	2 sts	4 sts
Row 11: Slip 1, P16, P2tog, P1, turn, leaving ____ unworked.	0 sts	2 sts

	WOMAN'S S–M	WOMAN'S L/ MAN'S M
Row 12: Slip 1, K17, ssk, K1, leaving ____ unworked.	0 sts	2 sts
Woman's S–M only: Heel turning complete. Do not turn to ws. You now have	20 sts	
Woman's L/Man's M only: **Row 13:** Slip 1, P18, P2tog, P1, leaving ____ unworked.		0 sts
Row 14: Slip 1, K19, ssk, K1, leaving ____ unworked.		0 sts
Woman's L/Man's M only: Heel turning complete. Do not turn to wrong side. You now have		22 sts
PICKING UP STITCHES FOR HEEL GUSSET		
Note: For techniques, see Secrets for Tight, Smooth Gussets, pages 26–29.		
Setup		
Using the needle with the remaining heel stitches (which will become Needle 4), pick up and knit ___ along right side of heel flap.	17 sts	19 sts
Needles 1 and 2: Knit to end of each needle.		
With empty needle (which will become Needle 3), pick up and knit ___ along left side of heel flap.	17 sts	19 sts
On same Needle 3, knit ___ from the heel stitches.	10 sts	11 sts
Needle 4: Knit the remaining heel stitches, plus picked up stitches from the right side of the the heel flap.		
You now have		
Needle 1:	16 sts	18 sts
Needle 2:	16 sts	18 sts
Needle 3:	27 sts	30 sts
Needle 4:	27 sts	30 sts
Total on all needles:	86 sts	96 sts
WORKING GUSSET DECREASES		
Round 1 Needles 1 and 2: Knit to end of each needle. Needle 3: K1, ssk, K to end of needle. Needle 4: Knit to last 3 sts, K2tog, K1.		
Round 2: Knit to end of each needle.		

	WOMAN'S S–M	WOMAN'S L/ MAN'S M
Next Rounds: Repeat Rounds 1 and 2 until each needle contains	16 sts	18 sts
Total on all needles:	64 sts	72 sts
WORKING THE SOCK FOOT		
Note: For a custom fit, you can make the sock longer or shorter by working more or fewer rounds for the foot.		
Knit to the end of each round until the sock measurement from the back of the heel is _____ or desired length.	7¾" (19.5cm)	8¼" (20.5cm)
SHAPING THE TOE		
Toe with contrasting stripe: Break off mc, leaving a tail for weaving, and use cc for first 6 rounds of toe, mc for next 4 rounds, and cc for remainder.		
Round 1 Needle 1: K1, ssk, K to end of needle. Needle 2: Knit to last 3 sts, K2tog, Kl. Needle 3: K1, ssk, K to end of needle. Needle 4: Knit to last 3 sts, K2tog, Kl.		
Round 2: Knit to end of each needle.		
Repeat Rounds 1 and 2 until you have a total of	12 sts	12 sts
CLOSING THE TOE AND FINISHING THE SOCK		
Setup: Slip the instep stitches on Needles 1 and 2 onto one needle and the sole stitches on Needles 3 and 4 onto another. Break yarn, leaving a 10" (25cm) tail. Using tail, graft front and back stitches together using Kitchener stitch. (See pages 29–30.)		
Weave in end after grafting toe. Weave in any other loose ends. To block, lightly mist or steam sock and pat into shape.		

Lacy Days

Three traditional Japanese, easy-to-learn lace patterns adorn these elegantly simple socks. Their stretchiness makes them fit well. The cuffs vary: traditional 1×1 ribbing, seed stitch, and a modified knit-purl ribbing.

Sizes	Child's medium (6–8); Woman's medium–large
Yarn	
Clouds:	***Child's M* (not shown):** Lorna's Laces Shepherd Sock Yarn, 80% superwash wool/20% nylon, fingering weight, 1.5 oz (43g)/ 215 yd (197m) skeins: 1 skein ***Woman's M–L* (A at right):** Crystal Palace Panda Silk, 52% bamboo/ 43% superwash merino wool/5% combed silk, fingering weight, 1.75 oz (50g)/204 yd (188m) skeins: 2 skeins Bamboo Green #3005
Dreams:	***Child's M* (B at right):** Louet Gems, Fingering Weight (Super Fine #1), 100% merino wool, 1.75 oz (50g)/185 yd (170m) skeins: l skein Terra Cotta 80-1472 ***Woman's M–L* (C at right):** Crystal Palace Panda Silk, 52% bamboo/ 43% superwash merino wool/5% combed silk, fingering weight, 1.75 oz (50g)/204 yd (188m) skeins: 2 skeins Bamboo Green #3005
Patchwork:	***Child's M* (D at right):** Regia 4-ply Sock Yarn, 75% new machine-washable wool/25% polyamide, fingering weight, 1.75 oz (50g)/ 228 yd (210m) skeins: 1 skein Natural #0600 ***Woman's M–L* (E at right):** Crystal Palace Panda Silk, 52% bamboo/ 43% superwash merino wool/5% combed silk, fingering weight, 1.75 oz (50g)/204 yd (188m) skeins: 2 skeins Bamboo Green #3005
Needles	
Clouds and Patchwork:	US #1 (2.25mm), *or size you need to obtain correct gauge:* set of 4 or 5 double-point needles, one 32–40" *OR* two 24" circular needles
Dreams:	***Child's M:*** US #0 (2.0mm), *or size you need to obtain correct gauge;* ***Woman's M–L:*** US #1 (2.25mm), *or size you need to obtain correct gauge,* and US #1.5 (2.5mm) for seed-stitch cuff only
Gauge	***Child's M:*** 30 stitches = 4" (10cm) in stockinette stitch ***Woman's M–L:*** 36 stitches = 4" (10cm) in stockinette stitch **Note:** Use smaller or larger needle to adjust sock (or cuff) size.
Other supplies	Tape measure, yarn needle, yarn and needle gauge
Abbreviations	**cc** = contrast color; **K** = knit; **K2tog** = knit 2 stitches together; **mc** = main color; **P** = purl; **P2tog** = purl 2 stitches together; **rs** = right side; **s2kp** = slip 2 sts together knitwise, knit 1, pass 2 slipped sts over knit stitch; **ssk** = slip, slip, knit the 2 slipped stitches together; **st(s)** = stitch(es); **ws** = wrong side; **YO** = yarn over

C DREAMS
B DREAMS
D PATCHWORK
E PATCHWORK
A CLOUDS

Pattern Stitches (see charts, page 122)

Clouds (multiple of 6 stitches)

Round 1: *P1, ssk, YO, K1, YO, K2tog; repeat from * to end.

Rounds 2, 3, and 4: *P1, K5; repeat from * to end.

Round 5: *K1, YO, K2tog, P1, ssk, YO; repeat from * to end.

Rounds 6, 7, and 8: *K3, P1, K2; repeat from * to end.

Dreams (multiple of 6 stitches)

Rounds 1, 2: Knit.

Round 3: Purl.

Round 4: *K2, YO, s2kp, YO, K1; repeat from *to end.

Patchwork (multiple of 10 stitches)

Rounds 1, 3, 5 and 7: *K2tog, YO, K1, YO, ssk, K5; repeat from * to end.

Rounds 2, 4, 6 and 8: Knit.

Rounds 9, 11, 13, and 15: *K 5, K2tog, YO, K1, YO, ssk; repeat from * to end.

Rounds 10, 12, 14, and 16: Knit.

GETTING STARTED	CHILD'S M	WOMAN'S M–L
Note: For instructions on joining cast-on stitches into a round, see Joining: Trading Places and Getting Ready to Work, page 16.		
CLOUDS		
Setup: Loosely cast on Divide stitches evenly on the needle(s). Join into a round, being careful not to twist stitches.	48 sts	60 sts
WORKING THE RIBBING		
Work P1, K2 ribbing until measurement from cast-on edge is about	1" (2.5cm)	1¼" (3cm)
Next 2 Rounds: *K3, P1, K2; repeat from * to end.		
WORKING THE SOCK LEG		
Work the Clouds Stitch Pattern until measurement from the cast-on edge is approximately	4½"–5" (11–12.5cm)	6" (15cm)
End with Round 2. Turn work.		

MAKING THE HEEL FLAP	CHILD'S M	WOMAN'S M–L
Note: The heel flap is worked back and forth on two needles or needle tips — not in the round. The instep stitches wait on their needle(s) until you use them again in Picking Up Stitches for Heel Gusset (page 114). Slip all heel stitches purlwise, with yarn in front on the wrong side and with yarn in back on right-side rows. Start working the heel flap on the wrong side.		
Work the heel back and forth on the last	24 sts	30 sts
Row 1 (ws): Slip 1, P to end of heel stitches, turn to right side.		
Row 2 (rs): *Slip 1, K1; repeat from * to end of heel stitches.		
Repeat Rows 1 and 2 until the heel flap measures approximately	1½"–1¾" (4–4.5cm)	2½" (6cm)
End having just worked a right-side row.		
TURNING THE HEEL		
Note: Beginning on wrong side, turn the heel as follows, slipping all slipped stitches purlwise with yarn in front on wrong side and yarn in back on right side.		
Row 1 (ws): Slip 1, ___, P2tog, P1, turn, leaving ___ unworked.	P12 8 sts	P16 10 sts
Row 2 (rs): Slip 1, ___, ssk, K1, turn, leaving ___ unworked.	K3 8 sts	K5 10 sts
Row 3: Slip 1, ___, P2tog, P1, turn, leaving ___ unworked.	P4 6 sts	P6 8 sts
Row 4: Slip 1, ___, ssk, K1, turn, leaving ___ unworked.	K5 6 sts	K7 8 sts
Row 5: Slip 1, ___, P2tog, P1, turn, leaving ___ unworked.	P6 4 sts	P8 6 sts
Row 6: Slip 1, ___, ssk, K1, turn, leaving ___ unworked.	K7 4 sts	K9 6 sts

	CHILD'S M	WOMAN'S M–L
Row 7: Slip 1, ___, P2tog, P1, turn, leaving ___ unworked.	P8 2 sts	P10 4 sts
Row 8: Slip 1, ___, ssk, K1, turn, leaving ___ unworked.	K9 2 sts	K11 4 sts
Row 9: Slip 1, ___, P2tog, P1, turn, leaving ___ unworked.	P10 0 sts	P12 2 sts
Row 10: Slip 1, ___, ssk, K1, leaving ___ unworked.	K11 0 sts	K13 2 sts
Child's M only: Heel turning complete. You now have	14 sts	
Woman's M–L only: **Row 11:** Slip 1, ___, P2tog, P1, turn, leaving ___ unworked.		P14 0 sts
Row 12: Slip 1, ___, ssk, K1, leaving ___ unworked.		K15 0 sts
Woman's M–L only: Heel turning complete. You now have		18 sts
PICKING UP STITCHES FOR HEEL GUSSET		
Note: For techniques, see Secrets for Tight, Smooth Gussets, pages 26–29. See also chart, page 120.		
Setup		
Pick up and knit along the right edge of the heel flap	15 sts	19–21 sts
Work across all instep stitches beginning with Row 3 of pattern.		
Pick up and knit ____ along the heel flap's left edge	15 sts	19–21 sts
Gusset stitches pick-up complete. You now have	68 sts	86–90 sts
Proceed to Working Gusset Decreases (page 120).		

DREAMS

Note: Use the larger needle to cast on stitches for Woman's medium/large. Child's medium is worked with one needle size throughout.		

	CHILD'S M	WOMAN'S M–L
Setup: Loosely cast on Divide stitches evenly among the needle(s). Join into a round, being careful not to twist stitches.	48 sts	60 sts
WORKING THE CUFF		
Note: For *Woman's M–L only*, use the larger needle to work the seed-stitch cuff. Other than this, the cuff is worked the same for both the child's and the woman's sock.		
Round 1: Work K1, P1 on all stitches.		
Round 2: Work P1, K1 on all stitches.		
Repeat Rounds 1 and 2 until cuff measures approximately ¾" for both the child's and the woman's sock.		
WORKING THE SOCK LEG		
Note: For *Woman's M–L only*, change back to the smaller needle(s) to work the leg and remainder of the sock.		
Work the Dreams Stitch Pattern until measurement from the cast-on edge is approximately	4½"–5" (11–12.5cm)	6" (15cm)
End with Round 2 and move 1 stitch from the heel to the instep in middle of the round. Turn work.		
MAKING THE HEEL FLAP		
Note: The heel flap is worked back and forth on two needles or needle tips — not in the round. The instep stitches wait on their needle(s) until you use them again in Picking Up Stitches for Heel Gusset (page 117). Slip all heel stitches purlwise, with yarn in front on the wrong side and with yarn in back on right-side rows. Start working the heel flap on the wrong side.		
Work the heel on	23 sts	29 sts
Row 1 (ws): Slip 1, P to end of heel stitches, turn to right side.		
Row 2 (rs): *Slip 1, K1; repeat from * to the last stitch, K1.		

	CHILD'S M	WOMAN'S M–L
Repeat Rows 1 and 2 until the heel flap measures approximately	1½"–1¾" (4–4.5cm)	2½" (6cm)
End having just worked a right-side row.		
TURNING THE HEEL		
Note: Beginning on wrong side, turn the heel as follows, slipping all slipped stitches purlwise with yarn in front on wrong side and yarn in back on right side.		
Row 1 (ws): Slip 1, ___, P2tog, P1, turn, leaving ___ unworked.	P11 8 sts	P15 10 sts
Row 2 (rs): Slip 1, ___, ssk, K1, turn, leaving ___ unworked.	K2 8 sts	K4 10 sts
Row 3: Slip 1, ___, P2tog, P1, turn, leaving ___ unworked.	P3 6 sts	P5 8 sts
Row 4: Slip 1, ___, ssk, K1, turn, leaving ___ unworked.	K4 6 sts	K6 8 sts
Row 5: Slip 1, ___, P2tog, P1, turn, leaving ___ unworked.	P5 4 sts	P7 6 sts
Row 6: Slip 1, ___, ssk, K1, turn, leaving ___ unworked.	K6 4 sts	K8 6 sts
Row 7: Slip 1, ___, P2tog, P1, turn, leaving ___ unworked.	P7 2 sts	P9 4 sts
Row 8: Slip 1, ___, ssk, K1, turn, leaving ___ unworked.	K8 2 sts	K10 4 sts
Row 9: Slip 1, ___, P2tog, P1, turn, leaving ___ unworked.	P9 0 sts	P11 2 sts
Row 10: Slip 1, ___, ssk, K1, turn, leaving ___ unworked.	K10 0 sts	K12 2 sts
Child's M only: Heel turning complete. You now have	13 sts	
Woman's M–L only: **Row 11:** Slip 1, ___, P2tog, P1, turn, leaving ___ unworked.		P13 0 sts

	CHILD'S M	WOMAN'S M–L
Row 12: Slip 1, ___, ssk, K1. You now have		K14 17 sts
Woman's M–L only: Heel turning complete.		
PICKING UP STITCHES FOR HEEL GUSSET		
NOTE: For techniques, see Secrets for Tight, Smooth Gussets, pages 26–29. See also chart, page 120.		
SETUP		
Pick up and knit along the right edge of the heel flap	15 sts	19 sts
Work across all instep stitches, beginning with Row 4 of Dreams Stitch Pattern. Because of the extra balancing stitch added, you will end in K2, not K1.		
Pick up and knit along the heel flap's left edge	15 sts	19–21 sts
Gusset stitches pick-up complete. You now have	68 sts	86–90 sts
Proceed to Working Gusset Decreases (page 120).		

PATCHWORK

	CHILD'S M	WOMAN'S M–L
SETUP: Loosely cast on	50 sts	60 sts
Divide stitches evenly on the needle(s). Join into a round, being careful not to twist stitches.		
WORKING THE RIBBING		
Work K1, P1 ribbing until measurement from cast-on edge is be about	¾" (2cm)	1" (2.5cm)
WORKING THE SOCK LEG		
Work the Patchwork Stitch Pattern until measurement from the cast-on edge is approximately	4½"–5" (11–12.5cm)	6" (15cm)
End with ____. Turn work.	Rnd 15	Rnd 7 or 15

MAKING THE HEEL FLAP	CHILD'S M	WOMAN'S M–L
Note: The heel flap is worked back and forth on two needles or needle tips — not in the round. The instep stitches wait on their needle(s) until you use them again in Picking Up Stitches for Heel Gusset (page 119). Slip all heel stitches purlwise, with yarn in front on the wrong side and with yarn in back on right-side rows. Start working the heel flap on the wrong side.		
Work the heel on	23 sts	30 sts
Child's M only: In the first heel flap row, decrease 2 heel stitches by working a P2tog in the 5 stitches closest to the beginning of the row and by working a P2tog in the 5 stitches closest to the end of the row.		
Row 1 (ws): Slip 1, P to end of heel stitches, turn to right side.		
Row 2 (rs) *Child's M only:* *Slip 1, K1; repeat from * to the last stitch, K1. *Woman's M–L only:* *Slip 1, K1; repeat from * to end of heel stitches.		
Repeat Rows 1 and 2 until the heel flap measures approximately	1½"–1¾" (4–4.5cm)	2½" (6cm)
End having just worked a right-side row.		
TURNING THE HEEL		
Note: Beginning on wrong side, turn the heel as follows, slipping all slipped stitches purlwise with yarn in front on wrong side and yarn in back on right side.		
Row 1 (ws): Slip 1, ___, P2tog, P1, turn, leaving ___ unworked.	P11 8 sts	P16 10 sts
Row 2 (rs): Slip 1, ___, ssk, K1, turn, leaving ___ unworked.	K2 8 sts	K5 10 sts
Row 3: Slip 1, ___, P2tog, P1, turn, leaving ___ unworked.	P3 6 sts	P6 8 sts
Row 4: Slip 1, ___, ssk, K1, turn, leaving ___ unworked.	K4 6 sts	K7 8 sts

	CHILD'S M	WOMAN'S M–L
Row 5: Slip 1, ___, P2tog, P1, turn, leaving ___ unworked.	P5 4 sts	P8 6 sts
Row 6: Slip 1, ___, ssk, K1, turn, leaving ___ unworked.	K6 4 sts	K9 6 sts
Row 7: Slip 1, ___, P2tog, P1, turn, leaving ___ unworked.	P7 2 sts	P10 4 sts
Row 8: Slip 1, ___, ssk, K1, turn, leaving ___ unworked.	K8 2 sts	K11 4 sts
Row 9: Slip 1, ___, P2tog, P1, turn, leaving ___ unworked.	P9 0 sts	P12 2 sts
Row 10: Slip 1, ___, ssk, K1, turn, leaving ___ unworked.	K10 0 sts	K13 2 sts
Child's M only: Heel turning complete. You now have	13 sts	
Woman's M–L only: **Row 11:** Slip 1, ___, P2tog, P1, turn, leaving ___ unworked.		P14 0 sts
Row 12: Slip 1, ___, ssk, K1, turn, leaving ___ unworked.		K15 0 sts
Heel turning complete. You now have		18 sts
PICKING UP STITCHES FOR HEEL GUSSET		
Note: For techniques, see Secrets for Tight, Smooth Gussets, pages 26–29. See also chart, page 120.		
Setup		
Pick up and knit along the right edge of the heel flap	15 sts	19–21 sts
Work across all instep stitches, beginning with either Row 8 or Row 16 of the Patchwork Stitch Pattern, depending on whether you ended with Row 7 or Row 15.		
Pick up and knit along the heel flap's left edge	15 sts	19–21 sts
Gusset stitches pick-up complete. You now have	68 sts	86–90 sts
Proceed to Working Gusset Decreases (page 120).		

Picking Up Stitches for Heel Gusset

As explained in Secrets for Tight, Smooth Gussets (pages 26–29), you may want to pick up more stitches, if needed, to avoid gaps and looseness along the heel flap edges. I pick up 1 stitch in every slipped stitch and occasionally add another 1 or so at the top to eliminate the pesky holes. The extras can be eliminated by knitting 2 stitches together where the last gusset stitches and the stitches that remained after turning come together or at the top of the gusset before working the first decrease round. Or you can just keep repeating gusset decrease rounds 1 and 2 until the original 48 or 60 total stitches are on the needle.

PATTERN/ SIZE	REMAINING	PICK UP/ RIGHT	PICK UP/ LEFT	INSTEP	TOTAL
Clouds					
Child's	14 sts	15 sts	15 sts	24 sts	68 sts
Woman's	18 sts	19–21 sts	19–21 sts	30 sts	86–90 sts
Dreams					
Child's	13 sts	15 sts	15 sts	25 sts	68 sts
Woman's	17 sts	19–21 sts	19–21 sts	31 sts	86–90 sts
Patchwork					
Child's	13 sts	15 sts	15 st	25 sts	68 sts
Woman's	18 sts	19–21 sts	19–21 sts	30 sts	86–90 sts

FOR ALL VERSIONS

WORKING GUSSET DECREASES	CHILD'S M	WOMAN'S M–L
Note: In this section, you will be working the chosen stitch pattern as established on the first half of the stitches (instep) and making the gusset decreases while knitting the remaining stitches (heel, which will become the sole).		
Round 1 Instep stitches: Work in pattern as established. Heel stitches: K1, ssk, K to last 3 heel stitches, K2tog, K1. (You have decreased 2 stitches.)		
Round 2 Instep stitches: Work in pattern as established. Heel stitches: Knit all stitches.		

	CHILD'S M	WOMAN'S M–L
Next Rounds: Repeat Rounds 1 and 2 until you have	48 sts	60 sts
WORKING THE SOCK FOOT		
Continue working without making further decreases, patterning instep stitches and knitting heel/sole stitches as established until 2" (5cm) less than desired foot length. Finished sock length measured from the back of the heel is approximately	4¼" (11cm)	8¼" (20.5cm)
Note: If you want the sock foot longer, but not as long as it would be if you worked another entire repeat before toe shaping (such as the 16 rows of Patchwork), you may instead work as many more rounds as desired in stockinette stitch to get the extra length.		
SHAPING THE TOE		
Note: If you are making Dreams or Patchwork in *Child's M,* now move 1 instep stitch back to the heel/sole stitches to equalize the number of stitches. The toes of each sock are shaped in the same manner using stockinette stitch (knitting every round). Now we are shaping the instep and bottom of the sole (same stitches as were earlier heel stitches).		
Setup		
For the instep, you have	24 sts	30 sts
For the sole, you have	24 sts	30 sts
Round 1: Knit all stitches to end of round.		
Round 2		
Instep stitches: K1, ssk, K to last 3 stitches, K2tog, K1.		
Sole stitches: K1, ssk, K to last 3 stitches, K2tog, K1.		
Round 3: Knit all stitches to end of round.		
Next Rounds: Repeat Rounds 2 and 3 until 16 stitches remain (8 instep and 8 sole/heel stitches).		

CLOSING THE TOE AND FINISHING THE SOCK	CHILD'S M	WOMAN'S M–L
Break yarn, leaving a 10" (25cm) tail. Hold the remaining stitches parallel on two needles or needle tips. Using the tail threaded on a yarn needle, graft front and back stitches together using Kitchener stitch (see pages 29–30). Weave in end after grafting toe. Weave in any other loose ends.		
To block, lightly mist or steam sock and pat gently into shape.		

Clouds

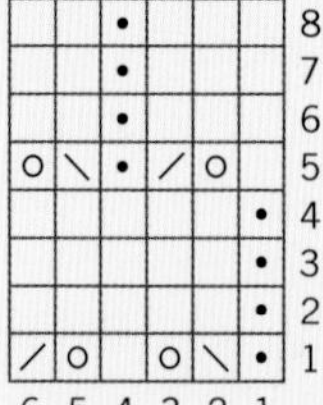

Dreams

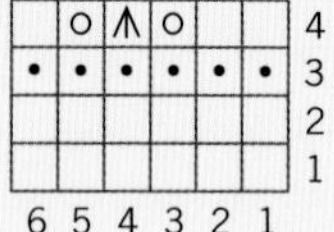

K KNIT

P PURL

YO YARN OVER

K2TOG KNIT 2 TOGETHER
knit 2 stitches together as one stitch

SSK SLIP, SLIP, KNIT
slip 1 stitch as if to knit, slip another stitch as if to knit, insert left-hand needle into front of these 2 stitches and knit them together

S2KP SKIP 2, KNIT, PASS
slip first and second stitches together as if to knit, knit 1 stitch, pass 2 slipped stitches over the knit stitch

Patchwork

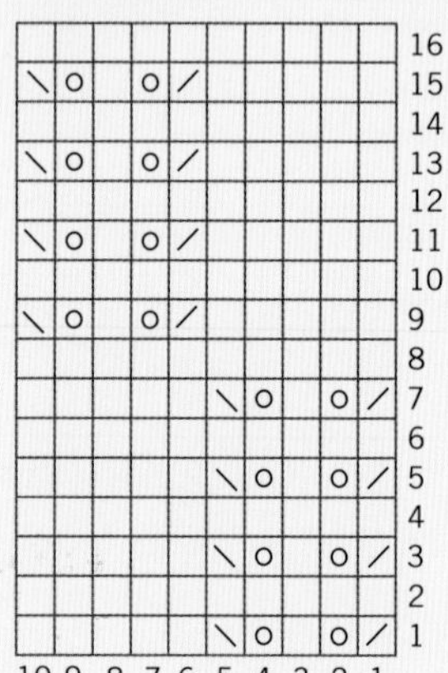

Splicing Ends Together

A quick and easy way to join old and new yarns is to spit-splice them together to avoid weaving in the ends. This is a timesaver for socks that have a number of different yarns and regular color changes. In addition, the join made is very smooth and strong. Here's how to do it:

Separate the plies in each of the yarn ends to be spliced. Really pick them apart for about 1"–1½" (2.5–4cm) as shown in the illustration. Bring the two ends together, so that the plies overlap and plies from the two ends are intermingled. Then moisten the area of the join with saliva until it is pretty wet (you don't really have to spit on it!). Next, put the join between the palms of your hands and rub them together vigorously. The overlapped area will get thinner and thinner until it is about the size of a single yarn end. The heat and friction from your palm rubbing the yarn ends has created a good strong spit-splice join, actually felting the ends together.

Note: The spit-splice method works only with wool and other natural fibers that will felt. Synthetics or wool yarn that has been treated so that it can be machine washed (for example, "superwash" yarn) cannot be spliced together in this way. Also, be sure to make the splice before you are actually out of yarn. You'll need at least a 6" (15cm) tail left and 6–8 stitches to go before starting the new color.

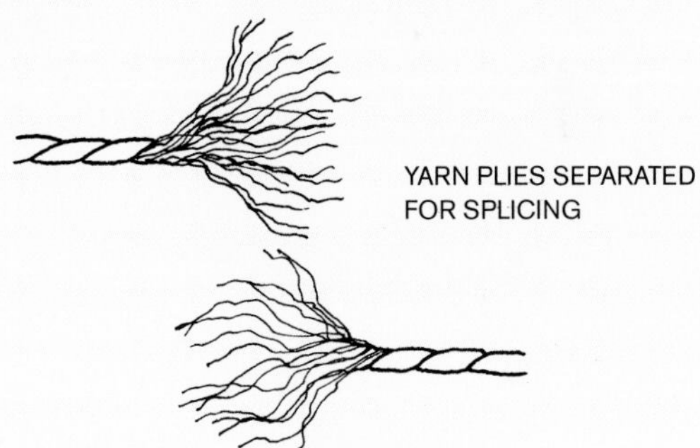

Fireside Stripes

Use your imagination to experiment with color, as you create these warm and wonderful socks knit with two strands of yarn. For a work of art you'll be proud to wear, pick your favorite hand-dyed or variegated yarn to use throughout and add three coordinating solids sequentially to make subtle stripes. You can also combine a solid color with three changing complementary colors. This fun technique offers an easy way to play with colors and a new world of sock possibilities. The Eye-of-Peacock stitch on the heel is especially nice.

Sizes	Woman's small–medium Woman's large/Man's medium
Yarn	Mountain Colors Weavers' Wool Quarters, 100% wool, DK, 3.5 oz (100g)/350 yd (320m) skeins 1 skein mc (Indian Corn) Cascade 220, 100% wool, worsted weight, 3.5 oz (100g)/220 yd (202m) skeins 115 yards cc1 (heather brown/#9408) 130 yards cc2 (brick red/#8884) 50 yards cc3 (copper/#2414) **Note:** Mc is used throughout sock along with one of the three cc yarns, which alternate to produce subtle striping.
Needles	One 5-needle set US #6 (4mm) double-point needles, *or size you need to obtain correct gauge*
Gauge	18 sts = 4" (10cm) in stockinette stitch
Other supplies	Tape measure, yarn needle, needle and stitch gauge
Abbreviations	**cc** = contrasting color yarn; **K**= knit; **K2tog** = knit 2 stitches together; **mc** = main color yarn; **P** = purl; **P2tog** = purl 2 stitches together; **rs** = right side; **ssk** = slip, slip, knit the 2 slipped stitches together; **St st** = stockinette stitch; **st(s)** = stitch(es); **ws** = wrong side; **wyb** = with yarn in back; **wyf** = with yarn in front

GETTING STARTED	WOMAN'S S–M	WOMAN'S L/ MAN'S M
Note: You will be holding 2 strands together throughout the sock, 1 strand of mc along with 1 strand of a cc yarn. You will find suggested measurements for the length of the ribbing, the sock leg, the heel flap, and the foot. Any of these measurements may be adjusted by working more or fewer rounds, if desired.		
Setup		
Using mc and cc1, loosely cast on	36 sts	40 sts
Divide stitches evenly onto 4 needles. On each needle you will have	9 sts	10 sts
Join into a round being careful not to twist stitches. (For instructions, see Joining: Trading Places and Getting Ready to Work, page 16.)		
Rounds begin and end on the right side of the sock foot as worn.		
WORKING THE RIBBING		
Using mc and cc1 held together, work K2, P2 ribbing for	1½" (4cm)	1¾" (4.5cm)
KNITTING THE SOCK LEG		
Note: To create the subtle stripes in the leg, you will be working 6 rounds of mc held with one of the cc yarns. Cc1 (used also for the ribbing) will be used for one St st stripe; cc2 and cc3 will each be used in two St st stripes (assuming that you do not adjust length of sock leg). An alternative to weaving in the ends when changing colors is spit splicing. (See instruction for this technique in the box on page 123, Splicing Ends Together.)		
Round 1: Continuing to use mc and cc1, knit to end of round. Break off cc1, leaving a tail for weaving in later.		
Rounds 2–7: Using mc and cc2, knit to end of each round.		
Break cc2, leaving tail for weaving in as above. Begin using cc3 with mc in next round. Alternatively, spit splice cc2 and cc3 to avoid having to weave in ends.		
Rounds 8–13: Using mc and cc3, knit to end of each round.		
Rounds 14–19: Using mc and cc1, knit to end of each round.		

	WOMAN'S S–M	WOMAN'S L/ MAN'S M
Repeat Rounds 2–19 until work measures 4½" (11cm) or desired length. Complete one of the 6-round stripes before beginning the heel.		
MAKING THE EYE-OF-PEACOCK HEEL FLAP		
SETUP Slip the stitches from Needles 3 and 4 onto a single needle to work the heel. Heel will be worked back and forth on these Break off cc currently in use. Turn work to wrong side.	18 sts	20 sts
Row 1: Using mc and cc2, slip 1 wyf, P ___, turn to rs.	17 sts	19 sts
Row 2: *K1, slip 1 wyb; repeat from * to last 3 stitches, slip 1, K2; turn to ws.		
Row 3: Slip l wyf, P___, turn to rs.	17 sts	19 sts
Row 4: *Slip 1 wyb, K1; repeat from * to end of row; turn to ws.		
Rows 5–20: Repeat Rows 1–4; heel flap will measure	2½" (6cm)	2¾" (7cm)
End heel flap by working Row 2 or Row 4 (right side rows) before beginning the heel.		
TURNING THE DUTCH, OR SQUARE, HEEL		
Beginning on wrong side, turn heel by working following rows:		
Row 1 (ws): ___, P2tog, turn, leaving 5 sts unworked.	P11	P13
Row 2 (rs): ___, ssk, turn, leaving 5 sts unworked.	K5	K7
Row 3: ___, P2tog, turn leaving 4 sts unworked.	P5	P7
Row 4: ___, ssk, turn, leaving 4 sts unworked.	K5	K7
Row 5: ___, P2tog, turn, leaving 3 sts unworked.	P5	P7
Row 6: ___, ssk, turn, leaving 3 sts unworked.	K5	K7
Row 7: ___, P2tog, turn, leaving 2 sts unworked.	P5	P7

	WOMAN'S S–M	WOMAN'S L/ MAN'S M
Row 8: ___, ssk, turn, leaving 2 sts unworked.	K5	K7
Row 9: ___, P2tog, turn, leaving 1 st unworked.	P5	P7
Row 10: ___, ssk, turn, leaving 1 st unworked.	K5	K7
Row 11: ___, P2tog, turn, leaving 0 sts unworked.	P5	P7
Row 12: ___, ssk, turn, leaving 0 sts unworked.	K5	K7
Heel turning complete. You now have	6 sts	8 sts
Break off cc2, leaving tail for weaving in later.		
PICKING UP STITCHES FOR HEEL GUSSET		
Note: For techniques, see Secrets for Tight, Smooth Gussets, pages 26–29.		
Setup	11 sts	12 sts
Use mc and needle holding heel stitches. Pick up and knit ___ along right side of heel flap.	18 sts	20 sts
Needles 1 and 2: Knit the ___ instep stitches.	11 sts	12 sts
With empty needle (this is now Needle 3), pick up and knit ___ along left side of heel flap.	3 sts	4 sts
On same Needle 3, knit ___ remaining after heel turning.		
With empty needle (this will be Needle 4), knit the remaining heel stitches and the stitches picked up on the right side of the heel flap.	9 sts	10 sts
You now have	9 sts	10 sts
Needle 1 (instep):	14 sts	16 sts
Needle 2 (instep):	15 sts	16 sts
Needle 3 (heel):	47 sts	52 sts
Needle 4 (heel):		
You have a total of:		
WORKING GUSSET DECREASES		
Using mc and cc1, work gusset decreases as follows:		
Round 1		
Needles 1 and 2: Knit to the end of each needle		
Needle 3: K1, ssk, K to end of needle.		
Needle 4: Knit to last 3 sts, K2tog, K1		

	WOMAN'S S–M	WOMAN'S L/ MAN'S M
Round 2: Knit to end of each needle.		
Repeat Rounds 1 and 2, maintaining color patterning, until each of the four needles contains	9 sts	10 sts
You now have	36 sts	40 sts
WORKING THE SOCK FOOT		
Making no further decreases, and continuing in color stripe patterning, knit to end of each round until 2" (5cm) from desired sock length, or until measurement from back of heel is approximately	8" (20cm)	8¼" (21cm)
Finish the last round at end of Needle 4 at right side.		
SHAPING THE TOE		
Using mc and cc2 (or desired cc), shape toe as follows: **Round 1** Needle 1: K1, ssk, K to end of needle. Needle 2: Knit to last 3 sts, K2tog, K1 Needle 3: K1, ssk, K to end of needle. Needle 4: Knit to last 3 sts, K2tog, K1.		
Round 2: Knit to end of round. You now have	32 sts	36 sts
Repeat Rounds 1 and 2 until there are 3 stitches on each of the four needles. You now have	12 sts	12 sts
CLOSING THE TOE AND FINISHING THE SOCK		
Setup: Slip the 3 stitches of Needle 1 onto Needle 2. Then slip the 3 stitches of Needle 3 onto Needle 4.		
Graft front and back stitches together using Kitchener stitch. (For instructions, see pages 29–30.)		
Weave in ends after grafting toe. Then weave in any other loose ends. To block, lightly mist or steam sock and pat into shape.		

Diamonds & Cables

Classic cables adorn these stretchy unisex socks. The larger size is worked in DK-weight yarn and features a sculptural center-front diamond cable. The smaller-sized version, a perfect introduction to knitting cables, is the basic garter rib and four-stitch cable combo, worked in fingering-weight yarn without the center diamond cable.

Sizes	**Cable and Garter (Fingering-Weight Version)** Woman's small–medium **Diamond Cable Garter (DK-Weight Version)** Woman's large/Man's medium
Yarn	**Cable & Garter Rib (Fingering-Weight Version) (shown on page 138)** Regia 4-ply Sock Yarn, 75% superwash wool/25% polyamide, fingering weight, 1.75 oz (50g)/228 yd (210m) skeins 2–3 skeins (depending upon sock size) Cherry #2002 **Note:** Depending on the length of foot and leg, 2 skeins may be adequate, but having 3 is safer. **Diamond Cable Rib (DK-Weight Version) (shown at right)** Regia 6-ply Sock Yarn, 75% superwash wool/25% polyamide, DK, 1.75 oz (50g)/136 yd (125m) skeins 3 skeins Denim #02137
Needles	**Cable & Garter Rib (Fingering-Weight Version)** US #1.5 (2.5mm), *or size you need to obtain correct gauge:* set of 4 or 5 double-point needles, one 32"–40" circular needle, *OR* two 24" circular needles **Diamond Cable Rib (DK-Weight Version)** US #2 (2.75mm), *or size you need to obtain correct gauge,* and US #1.5 (2.5mm) for toe shaping: set of 4 or 5 double-point needles, one 32"–40" circular needle, *OR* two 24" circular needles
Gauge	28 sts = 4" (10cm) in stockinette stitch
Other supplies	Tape measure, yarn needle, needle and stitch gauge, and cable needle the size of (or smaller than) the needles being used
Abbreviations	**cc** = contrast color; **K** = knit; **K2tog** = knit 2 stitches together; **mc** = main color; **P** = purl; **P2tog** = purl 2 stitches together; **rnd(s)** = round(s); **rs** = right side; **ssk** = slip, slip, knit the 2 slipped stitches together; **st(s)** = stitch(es); **ws** = wrong side

GETTING STARTED	FINGERING WT	DK WT
Note: In these patterns, the first stitches cast on and worked become the instep stitches and those remaining are the heel stitches. *For the Fingering Weight Version only,* a different number of stitches are worked for the instep (37 stitches) and for the heel (35 stitches). *For the DK Weight Version only,* use the larger needle to cast on stitches and work the sock leg.		
Setup: Loosely cast on	72 sts	74 sts
Divide stitches among the needles as follows:		
Instep needle(s):	37 sts	37 sts
Heel needle(s):	35 sts	37 sts
Join into a round, being careful not to twist stitches. (For instructions, see Joining: Trading Places and Getting Ready to Work, page 16.)		

Pattern Stitches

Fingering-Weight Version

Cable & Garter Ribbing

Instep (37 stitches): P1, (K1, P2, K2, P2, K1, P1) four times.

Heel (35 stitches): (K1, P2, K2, P2, K1, P1) three times, ending K1, P2, K2, P2, K1.

Cable & Garter

See Cable & Garter Chart on page 139.

DK-Weight Version

Diamond Cable Ribbing

Instep (37 stitches): K1, (P2, K2) 2 times; P1, (K2, P1) 6 times; (K2, P2) 2 times, K1.

Heel (37 stitches): P1, (K1, P2, K2, P2, K1, P1) 4 times.

Diamond Cable

See Diamond Cable Garter Chart on page 139.

Sizing Options

Go up or down in needle size to increase or decrease the circumference of these socks. To shorten the socks or use less yarn, work fewer pattern repeats for the leg and/or foot. The Diamond Cable DK-weight model has four leg and four foot pattern repeats; leg length from cast on to heel is approximately 8" (20cm) and foot length is approximately 11" (28cm). The Cable & Garter fingering-weight model has five leg and four foot pattern repeats; leg length from cast on to heel is approximately 7½" (19cm) and foot length is approximately 9¾" (25cm).

WORKING THE RIBBING	FINGERING WT	DK WT
Work the appropriate sock's ribbing pattern for	10 rnds	12–14 rnds
Ribbing will measure approximately	1" (2.5cm)	1¼"–1½" (3–4cm)
WORKING THE SOCK LEG		
Fingering Weight only: Work the full 37-stitch pattern on the instep and work *only* stitches 2–36 on the heel (35 heel stitches).		
Both weights: Work the appropriate 16-round pattern repeat a total of	5 times	4 times
The measurement from the cast-on edge is approximately	7½" (19cm)	8" (20cm)
MAKING THE HEEL FLAP		
Note: The heel flap is worked back and forth on two double-point needles or one circular needle — not in the round. The instep stitches wait on their needle(s) until you use them again in Picking Up Stitches for Heel Gusset (page 135). Slip all heel stitches purlwise, with yarn in front on the wrong side and with yarn in back on right-side rows. Start working the heel flap on the wrong side.		
Fingering Weight only: Work the heel flap back and forth on	35 sts	
Row 1 (ws): Slip 1, P to end of heel stitches, turn to right side.		

	FINGERING WT	DK WT
Row 2 (rs): *Slip 1, K1, repeat from * to last 3 stitches, S1, K2.		
Repeat Rows 1 and 2 until the heel flap measures approximately Rows 1 and 2 will be worked about End having just worked a right-side row.	2½" (6cm) 18 times	
DK Weight only: Begin working the heel flap on		37 sts
Row 1 (ws): Slip 1, P8, P2tog, P7, P2tog, P7, P2tog, P8. For the heel flap, you now have		34 sts
Row 2 (rs): *Slip 1, K1, repeat from * to end of heel stitches.		
Row 3 (ws): Slip 1, P to end of heel stitches.		
Repeat Rows 2 and 3 until the heel flap measures approximately 2½" (6cm) for the Woman's large or 2¾" (7cm) for the Man's medium. For *Woman's L,* Rows 2 and 3 will be worked about For *Man's M,* Rows 2 and 3 will be worked about End having just worked a right-side row.		15 times 17 times
TURNING THE HEEL		
Note: Beginning on wrong side, turn the heel as follows, slipping all slipped stitches purlwise with yarn in front on wrong-side rows and yarn in back on right-side rows.		
Begin turning the heel on	35 sts	34 sts
Row 1 (ws): Slip 1, ___, P2tog, P 1, turn, leaving ___ unworked.	P19 12 sts	P18 12 sts
Row 2 (rs): Slip 1, ___, ssk, K 1, turn, leaving ___ unworked.	K6 12 sts	K5 12 sts
Row 3: Slip 1, ___, P2tog, P1, turn, leaving ___ unworked.	P7 10 sts	P6 10 sts
Row 4: Slip 1, ___, ssk, K 1, turn, leaving ___ unworked.	K8 10 sts	K7 10 sts

	FINGERING WT	DK WT
Row 5: Slip 1, ___, P2tog, P 1, turn, leaving ___ unworked.	P9 8 sts	P8 8 sts
Row 6: Slip 1, ___, ssk, K1, turn, leaving ___ unworked.	K10 8 sts	K9 8 sts
Row 7: Slip l, ___, P2tog, P1, turn, leaving ___ unworked.	P11 6 sts	P10 6 sts
Row 8: Slip 1, ___, ssk, K1, turn, leaving ___ unworked.	K12 6 sts	K11 6 sts
Row 9: Slip 1, ___, P2tog, P 1, turn, leaving ___ unworked.	P13 4 sts	P12 4 sts
Row 10: Slip 1, ___, ssk, K1, turn, leaving ___ unworked.	K14 4 sts	K13 4 sts
Row 11: Slip 1, ___, P2tog, P1, turn, leaving ___ unworked.	P15 2 sts	P14 2 sts
Row 12: Slip 1, ___, ssk, K1, turn, leaving ___ unworked.	K16 2 sts	K15 2 sts
Row 13: Slip 1, ___, P2tog, P1, turn, leaving ___ unworked.	P17 0 sts	P16 0 sts
Row 14: Slip 1, ___, ssk, K1. Heel turning complete. You now have End having just worked a right-side row.	K18 21 sts	K17 20 sts
PICKING UP GUSSET STITCHES FOR HEEL GUSSET		
Note: For techniques, see Secrets for Tight, Smooth Gussets, pages 26–29. You want to pick up enough stitches to avoid holes or looseness along the edge of heel flap. To do this, as explained on page 27, you may want to pick up more stitches. I pick up 1 stitch in every slipped stitch and occasionally add another 1 or 2 at the top to eliminate the pesky holes. The extras can be eliminated by knitting 2 stitches together where the last gusset stitches and stitches that remained after turning come together or at top of the gusset before working first decrease round. Or you can just keep repeating gusset decrease Rounds 1 and 2 until back to the original number of stitches.		

	FINGERING WT	DK WT
SETUP		
Using the heel needle/needle tip, pick up and knit along the right edge of the heel flap	18 sts	17 sts
Starting with Row 1 of your chosen pattern and using the instep needle/needle tip, work across the instep's	37 sts	37 sts
Using the heel needle/needle tip, pick up and knit along the left edge of the heel flap	18 sts	17 sts
Working across the heel needle, knit	21 sts	20 sts
You now have		
Instep needle(s):	37 sts	37 sts
Heel/gusset needle(s):	57 sts	54 sts
Total on all needles:	94 sts	91 sts
WORKING GUSSET DECREASES		
Round 1		
Instep stitches: Work across in pattern as established.		
Heel/gusset stitches: K1, ssk, K to last 3 heel stitches, K2tog, K1. (You have decreased 2 stitches.)		
Round 2		
Instep stitches: Work in pattern as established.		
Heel/gusset stitches: Knit all stitches.		
Next Rounds: Repeat Rounds 1 and 2 until you have	72 sts	71 sts
Instep needle(s):	37sts	37 sts
Heel/gusset needle(s):	35 sts	34 sts
WORKING THE SOCK FOOT		
Continue working without making further decreases, patterning instep stitches and knitting heel/sole stitches as established. Work until measurement from the back of the heel is approximately 2½" (6cm) less than the desired finished sock length.		

SHAPING THE TOE	FINGERING WT	DK WT
Fingering Weight only:		
Setup		
Transfer 1 stitch from instep to heel before beginning toe shaping to equalize the number of stitches. You now have		
Instep needle(s):	36 sts	
Heel/sole needle(s):	36 sts	
Total on all needles:	72 sts	
Round 1		
Instep stitches: K1, ssk, K to last 3 stitches, K2tog, K1. You have decreased 2 stitches.		
Heel/sole stitches: K1, ssk, K to last 3 heel sts, K2tog, K1. You have decreased 2 stitches.		
You now have	68 sts	
Round 2: Knit all stitches on all needles.		
Next Rounds: Repeat Rounds 1 and 2 until 44 stitches remain (22 instep and 22 sole stitches). Half of the decreases have been worked.		
Next Rounds: Work Round 1 *only* every row until 16 stitches remain (8 instep and 8 sole stitches).		
DK Weight only:		
Setup:		
Transfer last instep stitch to heel/sole needle. You now have		
Instep needle(s):		36 sts
Heel needle(s):		35 sts
Total on all needles:		71 sts
Change to the smaller needle(s) to shape the toe. On Round 1, you need to decrease 1 extra stitch on the instep to equalize the number of stitches. After doing this, there will be 35 stitches on each needle.		
Round 1		
Instep stitches: K1, ssk, K15, K2tog, K to last 3 instep stitches, K2tog, K1. You have decreased 3 stitches.		
Heel/sole stitches: K1, ssk, K to last 3 heel stitches, K2tog, K1. You have decreased 2 stitches.You now have		66 sts
Round 2: Knit all stitches on all needles.		

	FINGERING WT	DK WT
Round 3 Instep stitches: K1, ssk, K to last 3 stitches, K2tog, K1. You have decreased 2 stitches. Heel/sole stitches: K1, ssk, K to last 3 stitches, K2tog, K1. You have decreased 2 more stitches.		
Next Rounds: Repeat Rounds 2 and 3 until 46 stitches remain (23 instep and 23 sole stitches). Half of the decreases have been worked.		
Next Rounds: Work Round 3 *only* every row until 14 stitches remain (7 instep and 7 sole stitches).		
CLOSING THE TOE AND FINISHING THE SOCK		
Break yarn, leaving a 10" (25cm) tail. Hold the remaining stitches parallel on two needles or needle tips. Using the tail threaded on a yarn needle, graft the front and back stitches together using Kitchener stitch (see pages 29–30). Weave in the end after grafting the toe. Weave in any other loose ends.		
To block, lightly mist or steam the sock and pat it gently into shape.		

Cable & Garter Chart

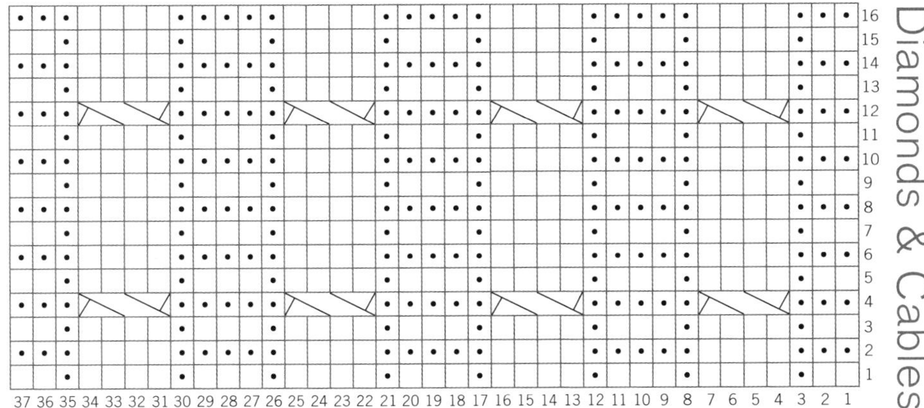

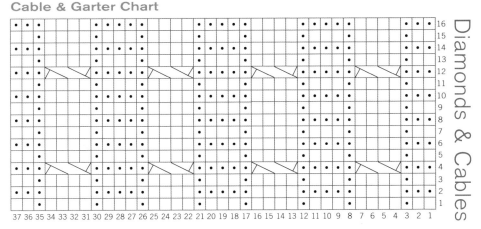

Diamond Cable Garter Chart

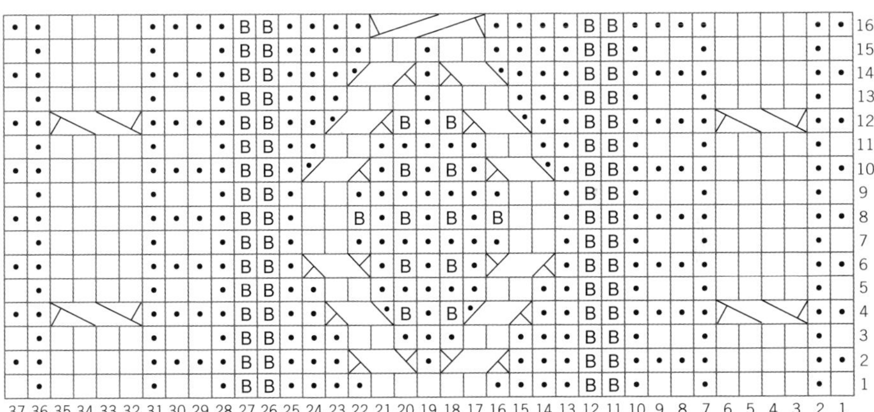

- K KNIT
- P PURL
- B **KNIT TBL** Knit stitch through back loop
- **C2 OVER 1 LEFT** slip 2 to cable needle, hold in front, K1, K2 from cable needle
- **C2 OVER 1 RIGHT** slip 1 to cable needle, hold in back, K2, K1 from cable needle
- **C2 OVER 1 RIGHT P** slip 1 to cable needle, hold in back, K2, P1 from cable needle
- **C2 OVER 1 LEFT P** slip 2 to cable needle, hold in front, P1, K2 from cable needle
- **C2 OVER 2 LEFT** slip 2 to cable needle, hold in front, K2, K2 from cable needle
- **C2 OVER 3 RIGHT** slip 3 to cable needle, hold in back, K2, then K3 from cable needle

Straight-Laced

Reveal a different side of your personality with lace socks that are simple to knit and fun to wear. This easy pattern knits up quickly and makes a stretchy sock that fits a variety of foot lengths — perfect for gift giving! Knit them in worsted- or fingering-weight yarns.

Size	Woman's medium–large. Stretches easily to fit shoe sizes 8½ to 10. Adjust foot length for smaller sizes.
Yarn	**Worsted-Weight Version (shown on page 149, left)** Cascade 220, 100% wool, 3.5 oz (100g)/220 yd (202m) skeins 1 skein Camel #835 **Fingering-Weight Version** Spud & Chloë Fine, 80% wool/20% silk, 2.3 oz (65g)/248 yd (227m) skeins 2 skeins Dachshund #7803 **(shown at right)** **Note:** One skein would make a pair of socks with a shorter leg and/or foot. Misti Alpaca Hand Paint, 50% alpaca/30% merino wool/10% silk/10% nylon, 3.5 oz (100g)/437 yd (400m) skeins 1 skein Bloodlines #HS02 **(shown on page 149, right)**
Needles	**Worsted-Weight Version:** One 5-needle set US #3 (3.25mm) double-point needles, *or size you need to obtain correct gauge* **Fingering-Weight Version:** (Spud & Chloë) One 5-needle set US #1.5 (2.5mm) double-point needles, *or size you need to obtain correct gauge* (Misti Alpaca Hand Paint) One 5-needle set US #1 (2.25mm) double-point needles, *or size you need to obtain correct gauge*
Gauge	**Worsted-Weight Version:** 24 sts = 4" (10cm) using mc in stockinette stitch **Fingering-Weight Version:** Spud & Chloë: 28 sts = 4" (10cm) in stockinette stitch; Misti Alpaca Hand Paint: 32 sts = 4" (10cm) in stockinette stitch
Other supplies	Tape measure, yarn needle, needle and stitch gauge
Abbreviations	**K** = knit; **K2tog** = knit 2 stitches together; **P** = purl; **P2tog** = purl 2 stitches together; **rs** = right side; **rnd(s)** = round(s); **ssk** = slip, slip, knit the 2 slipped stitches together; **st(s)** = stitch(es); **ws** = wrong side; **YO** = yarn over

WORKING THE RIBBING	WORSTED WT	FINGERING WT
Note: The beginning and end of each round will be on the right-hand side of the foot when the sock is being worn.		
Setup: Loosely cast on	40 sts	60 sts
If using double-pointed needles, divide stitches evenly among 4 needles. Each needle will contain	10 sts	15 sts
Join into a round, being careful not to twist stitches. (For instructions, see Joining: Trading Places and Getting Ready to Work, page 16.)		
(K1, P1, K1, P1, K1) ____ to end of each round for ribbing. Work the ribbing for 1"–1½" (2.5–3.75cm).	8 times	12 times
KNITTING THE SOCK LEG		
Note: The leg is worked in a Lace Pattern, which has 5 stitches in each pattern repeat.		
Round 1: Knit to end of each needle.		
Round 2: *K2tog, YO, K1, YO, ssk; repeat from *	7 more times	11 more times
Repeat Rounds 1 and 2 until measurement from cast-on edge is 5½" (13.75cm), about _______ (or until desired length to beginning of heel).	15 times	22 times
End by working Round 2.		
MAKING THE HEEL FLAP		
Note: This heel is worked in stockinette stitch with a narrow garter stitch edging on both sides of the heel flap. If desired, you can make the heel flap longer or shorter by working more or fewer rows. The heel stitches are worked back and forth on 2 needles/needle tips. Hold the instep stitches aside on Needles 1 and 2 while you work the heel flap. You now have		
Heel stitches:	20 sts	30 sts
Instep stitches:	20 sts	30 sts
Setup: Turn last needle used (Needle 4 or heel needle) around to wrong side to begin to work heel flap. On the first row, work all stitches onto one needle.		

	WORSTED WT	FINGERING WT
Row 1 (ws): K3, P___, K3, turn.	14 sts	24 sts
Row 2 (rs): Knit to end of needle, turn.		
Repeat Rows 1 and 2 until heel is approximately 2½" (6cm) or about	10 rows	14 rows
End by working a right-side row.		
TURNING THE HEEL		
Beginning on the wrong side, turn the heel as follows: **Row 1:** ___, P2tog, turn, leaving ____ unworked.	P13 5 sts	P20 8 sts
Row 2: ___, ssk, turn, leaving ____ unworked.	K7 5 sts	K11 8 sts
Row 3: ___, P2tog, turn, leaving ____ unworked.	P7 4 sts	P11 7 sts
Row 4: ___, ssk, turn, leaving ____ unworked.	K7 4 sts	K11 7 sts
Row 5: ___, P2tog, turn, leaving ____ unworked.	P7 3 sts	P11 6 sts
Row 6: ___, ssk, turn, leaving ____ unworked.	K7 3 sts	K11 6 sts
Row 7: ___, P2tog, turn, leaving ____ unworked.	P7 2 sts	P11 5 sts
Row 8: ___, ssk, turn, leaving ____ unworked.	K7 2 sts	K11 5 sts
Row 9: ___, P2tog, turn, leaving ____ unworked.	P7 1 st	P11 4 sts
Row 10: ___, ssk, turn, leaving ____ unworked.	K7 1 st	K11 4 sts
Row 11: ___, P2tog, turn, leaving ____ unworked.	P7 0 sts	P11 3 sts

	WORSTED WT	FINGERING WT
Row 12: ___, ssk. Unworked stitches:	K7 0 sts	K11 3 sts
Worsted Weight only: Heel turning complete. Do not turn. The heel contains	8 sts	
Fingering Weight only: Continue with rows 13–18 to complete heel turning.		
Row 13: ___, P2tog, turn, leaving ____ unworked.		P11 2 sts
Row 14: ___, ssk, turn, leaving ____ unworked.		K11 2 sts
Row 15: ___, P2tog, turn, leaving ____ unworked.		P11 1 st
Row 16: ___, ssk, turn, leaving ____ unworked.		K11 1 st
Row 17: ___, P2tog, turn, leaving ____ unworked.		P11 0 sts
Row 18: ___, ssk, leaving ____ unworked.		K11 0 sts
Fingering Weight only: Heel turning complete. Do not turn. The heel contains		12 sts
PICKING UP STITCHES FOR HEEL GUSSET		
Setup		
Using needle/needle tip holding the remaining heel turning stitches (which will become Needle 4), pick up and knit ___ along right side of heel flap.	12 sts	16 sts
Needles 1 and 2: Work Lace Pattern Round 1 (knit all stitches) across instep stitches.		
With empty needle (which will become Needle 3 or heel needle if using circular), pick up and knit ___ along left side of heel flap.	12 sts	16 sts
On same Needle 3: knit ___ from the heel stitches (half of those remaining after heel turning).	4 sts	6 sts
Needle 4: Knit remaining heel stitches plus stitches picked up on right side of heel (see above).		

	WORSTED WT	FINGERING WT
You now have		
Needles 1 and 2 (instep):	10 sts each	15 sts each
Needles 3 and 4 (heel):	16 sts each	22 sts each
Total on all 4 needles:	52 sts	74 sts
WORKING GUSSET DECREASES		
Round 1		
Needles 1 and 2 (instep): Work Lace Pattern, maintaining pattern as established in Knitting the Sock Leg.		
Needle 3: K1, ssk, K to end of needle.		
Needle 4: Knit to last 3 sts, K2tog, K1.		
You now have	50 sts	72 sts
Round 2: Knit to end of round.		
Next Rounds: Repeat Rounds 1 and 2 until each needle contains	10 sts	15 sts
WORKING THE SOCK FOOT		
Continue working Lace Pattern Rounds 1 and 2 on Needles 1 and 2 and knitting to end of each needle on Needles 3 and 4 until measurement from desired total sock length is	1¼" (3cm)	1½" (4cm)
For woman's average, the measurement from the back of the heel will be	8¾" (22cm)	8½" (21.5cm)
End by working Round 1 of Lace Pattern (knit to end of each needle).		
SHAPING THE TOE		
Round 1		
Needle 1: K1, ssk, YO, ssk, work Lace Pattern to end of needle.		
Needle 2: Work Lace Pattern to last 5 sts, K2tog, YO, K2tog, K1.		
Needle 3: K1, ssk, K to end of needle.		
Needle 4: Knit to last 3 sts, K2tog, K1.		
You now have	36 sts	56 sts
Rounds 2, 4, 6: Knit to end of each needle.		

	WORSTED WT	FINGERING WT
Round 3 Needle 1: K1, ssk, K1, work Lace Pattern to end of needle. Needle 2: Work Lace Pattern to last 4 sts, K1, K2tog, K1. Needle 3: K1, ssk, K to end of needle. Needle 4: Knit to last 3 sts, K2tog, K1. You now have	32 sts	52 sts
Round 5 Needle 1: K1, ssk, work Lace Pattern to end of needle. Needle 2: Work Lace Pattern to last 3 sts, K2tog, K1. Needle 3: K1, ssk, K to end of needle. Needle 4: Knit to last 3 sts, K2tog K1. You now have	28 sts	48 sts
Worsted Weight only: **Round 7** Needle 1: K1, ssk, K2, YO, ssk. Needle 2: K2tog, YO, K2, K2tog, K1. Needle 3: K1, ssk, K to end of needle. Needle 4: Knit to last 3 sts, K2tog, K1. You now have	24 sts	
Rounds 8–10 Needle 1: K1, ssk, K to end of needle. Needle 2: Knit to last 3 sts, K2tog, K1. Needle 3: K1, ssk, K to end of needle. Needle 4: Knit to last 3 sts, K2tog, K1. After Round 10 you now have	12 sts	
Fingering Weight only: **Round 7** Needle 1: K1, ssk, K2, YO, ssk, work Lace Pattern to end of needle. Needle 2: Work Lace Pattern to last 7 sts, K2tog, YO, K2, K2tog, K1. Needle 3: K1, ssk, K to end of needle. Needle 4: Knit to last 3 sts, K2tog, K1. You now have		44 sts

	WORSTED WT	FINGERING WT
Rounds 8, 10, 12, 14, 16: Knit to end of each round.		
Round 9 Needle 1: K1, ssk, K1, YO, K2tog, work Lace Pattern to end of needle. Needle 2: Work Lace Pattern to last 6 sts, K2tog, YO, K1, K2tog, K1. Needle 3: K1, ssk, K to end. Needle 4: Knit to last 3 sts, K2tog, K1. You now have		40 sts
Round 11 Needle 1: K1, ssk, YO, ssk, work Lace Pattern to end of needle. Needle 2: Work Lace Pattern to last 5 sts, K2tog, YO, K2tog, K1. Needle 3: K1, ssk, K to end of needle. Needle 4: Knit to last 3 sts, K2tog, K1. You now have a total of		36 sts
Round 13 Needle 1: K1, ssk, K1, work Lace Pattern to end of needle. Needle 2: Work Lace Pattern to last 4 sts, K1, K2tog, K1. Needle 3: K1, ssk, K to end of needle. Needle 4: Knit to last 3 sts, K2tog, K2. You now have a total of		32 sts
Round 15 Needle 1: K1, ssk, work Lace Pattern to end of needle. Needle 2: Work Lace Pattern to last 3 sts, K2tog, K1. Needle 3: K1, ssk, K to end. Needle 4: Knit to last 3 sts, K2tog, K1. You now have		28 sts
Round 17 Needle 1: K1, ssk, K2, YO, ssk. Needle 2: K2tog, YO, K2, K2tog, K1. Needle 3: K1, ssk, K to end of needle. Needle 4: Knit to last 3 sts, K2tog, K1. You now have		24 sts

	WORSTED WT	FINGERING WT
Rounds 18–20 Needle 1: K1, ssk, K to end of needle. Needle 2: Knit to last 3 sts, K2tog, K1. Needle 3: K1, ssk, K to end of needle. Needle 4: Knit to last 3 sts, K2tog, K1 After Round 20, you have a total of		12 sts
CLOSING THE TOE AND FINISHING THE SOCK		
Setup: Slip the 3 stitches of Needle 1 onto Needle 2, then slip the 3 stitches of Needle 3 onto Needle 4. If you are using circular needles, each will have 6 stitches.		
Graft the 12 stitches together using Kitchener stitch. (For instructions, see pages 29–30.) Weave in end after grafting toe. Weave in any other loose ends. To block, lightly mist or steam sock and pat gently to shape.		

Reinforcing Socks

You can make your socks more durable by knitting in a strand of reinforcing yarn or thread. You hold the reinforcement together with the regular sock yarn as the parts are being knit. Some sock parts often reinforced are the heel flap, heel cap or turning, and the toe. You may also wish to reinforce other parts that receive hard wear, such as the ball of the foot and the extension onto the sole of the stitches that remained after turning the heel. Doing this is an optional procedure, as even 100% wool socks knit to a dense gauge live on for years without this reinforcement.

Peaks 'n' Valleys

Combine a simple chevron lace stitch with self-striping or variegated yarns for a new slant on lace. The two-row repeat lace pattern is easy to learn and creates an attractive, stretchy sock that fits well. Another good beginning lace project! As an alternative, use two or more solid-colored yarns to create your own striping pattern.

Sizes	Woman's medium–large Infant 0–9 months
Yarn	**Woman's socks** Lana Grossa Meilenweit Cotton Fun, 45% cotton/42% wool/13% polyamid, fingering weight, 1.75 oz (50g)/208 yd (190m) skeins 2 skeins Yellow Multi #337 NOTE: Depending upon length of foot and leg, 2 skeins may be adequate for woman's socks done entirely in self-striping yarn, but having 3 skeins is safer, so you can ensure the striping on socks matches. **Infant's socks (not shown)** Regia Ringel Color, 75% wool/25% polyamide, fingering weight, 1.75 oz (50g)/230 yd (210m) skeins 1 skein Colibri/#5072 (enough for 2 pairs)
Needles	One 5-needle set US #1 (2.25mm) or US #1.5 (2.5mm) double-point needles, *or size you need to obtain correct gauge*
Gauge	30 sts = 4" (10cm) in stockinette stitch
Other supplies	Tape measure, yarn needle, needle and stitch gauge
Abbreviations	**K** = knit; **K2tog** = knit 2 stitches together; **P** = purl; **P2tog** = purl 2 stitches together; **rs** = right side; **ssk** = slip, slip, knit the 2 slipped stitches together; **st(s)** = stitch(es); **ws** = wrong side; **YO** = yarn over

GETTING STARTED	WOMAN'S M–L	INFANT
Setup: Loosely cast on	72 sts	36 sts
Divide stitches evenly among 4 needles. On each needle you will have	18 sts	9 sts
Join into a round, being careful not to twist stitches. (For instructions, see Joining: Trading Places and Getting Ready to Work, page 16.) Rounds begin and end at right side of heel as sock is worn.		
Round 1: Purl to end of round.		
Round 2: Knit to end of round.		
WORKING THE LEG		
Note: The leg and top of foot (instep) down to toe decrease are worked in the Lace Pattern, which is a 9-stitch, 2-row repeat (Rounds 1 and 2 below). You may adjust the leg length by working more or fewer rounds, as desired.		
Round 1: *Pl, ssk, K1, YO, K1, YO, K1, K2tog, P1; repeat from * to end of round. On each needle, you will be making	2 pattern repeats	1 pattern repeat
Round 2: *P1, K7, P1; repeat from * to end of round.		
Next Rounds: Repeat Rounds 1 and 2 (Lace Pattern) until measurement from cast-on edge is	6½" (16cm)	3" (8cm)
Final Round: Repeat Round 1.		
MAKING THE HEEL FLAP		
Note: When making the heel flap and turning the heel, slip all stitches with yarn in back on right-side rows and with yarn in front on wrong-side rows.		
Setup: Turn work to wrong side to begin the heel flap back. Slip all stitches from Needle 4 onto Needle 3, so that you can work back and forth using 2 needles. Stitches on Needles 1 and 2 (instep stitches) wait until the heel flap is complete. You will be working on	36 sts	18 sts
Row 1: Slip l, P___, turn work.	35 sts	17 sts
Row 2: *Slip 1, K1; repeat from * to end of row.		
Repeat Rows 1 and 2 ____ more times. Measurement of heel will be approximately	17 2½" (6cm)	8 1¼" (3cm)

TURNING THE HEEL	WOMAN'S M–L	INFANT
Row 1 (ws): Slip 1, ___, P2tog, P1, turn, leaving ___ unworked.	P20 12 sts	P10 4 sts
Row 2 (rs): Slip 1, ___, ssk, K1, turn, leaving _____ unworked.	K7 12 sts	K5 4 sts
Row 3: Slip 1, ___, P2tog, P1, turn, leaving _____ unworked.	P8 10 sts	P6 2 sts
Row 4: Slip 1, ___, ssk, K1, turn, leaving _____ unworked.	K9 10 sts	K7 2 sts
Row 5: Slip 1, ___, P2tog, P1, turn, leaving _____ unworked.	P10 8 sts	P8 0 sts
Row 6: Slip 1, ___, ssk, K1, turn, leaving _____ unworked. *Infant's heel turning complete.* You now have	K11 8 sts	K9 0 sts 12 sts
Woman's M–L only: **Row 7:** Slip 1, P12, P2tog, P1, turn, leaving ____ unworked.	6 sts	
Row 8: Slip 1, K13, ssk, K1, turn, leaving ____ unworked.	6 sts	
Row 9: Slip 1, P14, P2tog, P1, turn, leaving ____ unworked.	4 sts	
Row 10: Slip 1, K15, ssk, K1, turn, leaving ____ unworked.	4 sts	
Row 11: Slip 1, P16, P2tog, P1, turn, leaving ____ unworked.	2 sts	
Row 12: Slip 1, K17, ssk, K1, turn, leaving ____ unworked.	2 sts	
Row 13: Slip 1, P18, P2tog, P1, turn, leaving ____ unworked.	0 sts	
Row 14: Slip 1, K19, ssk, K1, leaving _____ unworked.	0 sts	
Woman's heel turning complete. You now have	22 sts	
PICKING UP STITCHES FOR HEEL GUSSET		
Note: Pick up more stitches if needed to avoid holes along heel flap. (For instructions see Secrets for Tight, Smotth Gussets, pages 26–29.)		

	WOMAN'S M–L	INFANT
Setup		
With empty needle, pick up and knit ___ along right side of heel flap.	18 sts	10 sts
Needles 1 and 2 (instep stitches): *P1, K7, P1; repeat from * to end of each needle.		
With empty needle, pick up and knit ___ along left side of heel flap. This is now Needle 3.	18 sts	10 sts
On same needle, knit ___ from the heel stitches (half of those remaining after heel turning).	11 sts	6 sts
Needle 4: Knit the remaining heel stitches, plus the stitches picked up on the right side of the heel flap.		
You now have		
Needle 1:	18 sts	9 sts
Needle 2:	18 sts	9 sts
Needle 3:	29 sts	16 sts
Needle 4:	29 sts	16 sts
Total on all 4 needles:	94 sts	50 sts
WORKING GUSSET DECREASES		
Round 1		
Needles 1 and 2: *Pl, ssk, K1, YO, K1, YO, K1, K2tog, P1; repeat from * to end of each needle.		
Needle 3: K1, ssk, K to end of needle.		
Needle 4: Knit to last 3 sts, K2tog, K1.		
You now have	92 sts	48 sts
Round 2		
Needles 1 and 2: *P1, K7, P1; repeat from * to end of each needle.		
Needles 3 and 4: Knit to end of each needle.		
Next Rounds: Repeat Rounds 1 and 2 until each needle contains	18 sts	9 sts
Gusset is complete and you now have	72 sts	36 sts
WORKING THE SOCK FOOT		
Note: You may adjust the foot length by working more or fewer rounds, as desired. Making no further decreases, continue the Lace Pattern on the instep stitches as established.		

	WOMAN'S M–L	INFANT
Round 1 Needles 1 and 2: *Pl, ssk, K1, YO, K1, YO, K1, K2tog, P1; repeat from * to end of each needle. Needles 3 and 4: Knit to end of each needle.		
Round 2 Needles 1 and 2: *P1, K7, P1; repeat from * to end of each needle. Needles 3 and 4: Knit to end of each needle.		
Repeat Rounds 1 and 2 until measurement from back of heel is	8¼" (21cm)	2¾" (7cm)
Note: Try on sock to determine length. Lace stretches, making it easy to make a sock too long. The toe adds to foot length about	1¾" (4.5cm)	1" (2.5cm)
SHAPING THE TOE		
Round 1 Needle 1: K1, ssk, K to end of needle. Needle 2: Knit to last 3 sts, K2tog, K1. Needle 3: K1, ssk, K to end of needle. Needle 4: Knit to last 3 sts, K2tog, K1. You now have	68 sts	32 sts
Round 2: Knit to end of each needle.		
Next Rounds: Repeat Rounds 1 and 2 until you have Each needle now has	44 sts 11 sts	24 sts 6 sts
Next Rounds: Repeat Round 1 Each needle now has 4 stitches (16 stitches total).	7 times	2 times
CLOSING THE TOE AND FINISHING THE SOCK		
Slip the 8 instep stitches of Needles 1 and 2 onto a single needle and the 8 sole stitches of Needles 3 and 4 onto another needle. Break yarn, leaving a 8–10" (20–25cm) tail for closing toe. Holding the two needles parallel, graft stitches together using Kitchener stitch, pages 29–30.) Weave in all loose ends. To block, lightly mist or steam sock and pat into shape.		

Simple Ribs

These great-fitting unisex socks can be made in both worsted- and DK-weight yarns. The ribbing creates a comfortable, stretchy sock that fits a variety of foot widths – a can't-miss pattern when making a surprise gift for someone you don't want to (or can't) measure.

Size	Woman's large/Man's medium
Yarn	**Single Rib (DK Weight) (at right on facing page)** Regia 6-ply Kaffe Fassett Design Line, 75% new wool/25% polyamide, DK, 1.75 oz (50g)/136 yd (125m) skeins 3 skeins Landscape Fire #5950 **Note:** Depending upon length of foot and leg, 2 skeins may be adequate, but having 3 is safer to be able to make striping on socks match. **Double Rib (Worsted Weight) (at left on facing page)** Cascade 220, 100% wool, worsted weight, 3.5 oz (100g)/220 yd (202m) skeins 2 skeins Turquoise heather/#9455
Needles	US #3 (3.25mm), *or size you need to obtain correct gauge:* set of 5 double-point needles, one 32"–40" circular needle, *OR* two 24" circular needles
Gauge	24 sts = 4" (10cm) in stockinette stitch
Other supplies	Tape measure, yarn needle, needle and stitch gauge
Abbreviations	**K** = knit; **k2tog** = knit 2 stitches together; **P** = purl; **P2tog** = purl 2 stitches together; **rs** = right side; **ssk** = slip, slip, knit the 2 slipped stitches together; **st(s)** = stitch(es); **ws** = wrong side; **wyb** = with yarn in back; **wyf** = with yarn in front

GETTING STARTED	DK WT (SINGLE RIB)	WORSTED WT (DOUBLE RIB)
Setup		
Loosely cast on	56 sts	48 sts
Divide stitches evenly among 4 needles. On each needle you will have	14 sts	12 sts
Join into a round, being careful not to twist stitches. (For instructions, see Joining: Trading Places and Getting Ready to Work, page 16.)		
Note: This sock starts and ends on the right-hand side of the sock foot as worn. If you are using circular needles, you will have 28 instep stitches and 28 heel/sole stitches for *Single Rib Pattern,* and 24 instep stitches and 24 heel/sole stitches for *Double Rib Pattern.*		
WORKING THE RIBBING AND LEG		
K1, P1 to end of each round until piece measures	5¾" (14.5cm)	¾" (2cm)
Double Rib only: P1, *K2, P2; repeat from * to last stitch, P1. Work this pattern each round for		6" (15cm)
MAKING THE HEEL FLAP		
Note: Add reinforcing thread here, if desired. (See page 148 for instructions.) For making and turning the heel, slip the slipped stitches purlwise with yarn in back (wyb) on right-side rows and with yarn in front (wyf) on wrong-side rows. The instep stitches that are on Needles 1 and 2 wait while you work the heel flap.		
Setup: Slip the stitches from Needle 3 onto Needle 4. Heel will be worked back and forth on these	28 sts	24 sts
Row 1: Turn work to wrong side. Slip 1, purl to end of row, turn.		
Row 2: *Slip 1, K1; repeat across from *, turn.		
Rows 3–24: Repeat Rows 1 and 2.		
Heel flap will be approximately 2½" (6cm) long.		

TURNING THE HEEL	DK WT (SINGLE RIB)	WORSTED WT (DOUBLE RIB)
Note: Row 1 begins on wrong side.		
Row 1 (ws): Slip 1, ___, P2tog, P1, turn, leaving ___ unworked.	P14 10 sts	P14 6 sts
Row 2 (rs): Slip 1, ___, ssk, K1, turn, leaving ___ unworked.	K3 10 sts	K7 6 sts
Row 3: Slip 1, ___, P2tog, P1, turn, leaving ___ unworked.	P4 8 sts	P8 4 sts
Row 4: Slip 1, ___, ssk, K1, turn, leaving ___ unworked.	K5 8 sts	K9 4 sts
Row 5: Slip 1, ___, P2tog, P1, turn, leaving ___ unworked.	P6 6 sts	P10 2 sts
Row 6: Slip 1, ___, ssk, K1, turn, leaving ___ unworked.	K7 6 sts	K11 2 sts
Row 7: Slip 1, ___, P2tog, P1, turn, leaving ___ unworked.	P8 4 sts	P12 0 sts
Row 8: Slip 1, ___, ssk, K1, turn, leaving ___ unworked.	K9 4 sts	K13 0 sts
Double Rib Pattern (Worsted weight): Heel turning complete. You now have		16 sts
Single Rib Pattern (DK weight) only: **Row 9:** Slip 1, P __, P2tog, P1, turn, leaving ___ unworked.	P10 2 sts	
Row 10: Slip 1, ___, ssk, K1, turn, leaving ___ unworked.	K11 2 sts	
Row 11: Slip 1, ___, P2tog, P1, turn, leaving ___ unworked.	P12 0 sts	
Row 12: Slip 1, ___, ssk, K1, turn, leaving ___ unworked.	K13 0 sts	
Single Rib Pattern (DK weight): Heel turning complete. You now have	16 sts	

PICKING UP THE STITCHES FOR HEEL GUSSET	DK WT (SINGLE RIB)	WORSTED WT (DOUBLE RIB)
Note: Pick up 1 or 2 more stitches if needed to avoid holes along heel flap. (See Secrets for Tight, Smooth Gussets, pages 26–29.)		
Setup: With empty needle, pick up and knit ___ along right side of heel flap.	13 sts	12 sts
Needles 1 and 2 (instep stitches): Work *Single* or *Double Rib Pattern* as established across	28 sts	24 sts
With empty needle, pick up and knit 12 stitches along left side of heel flap. Continuing with same needle, knit half of the heel stitches	8 sts	8 sts
With empty needle, knit remaining half of the heel stitches	8 sts	8 sts
Continuing with same needle, knit the 12 picked up stitches on the right side of heel flap.		
You now have		
Needle 1:	14 sts	12 sts
Needle 2:	14 sts	12 sts
Needle 3:	20 sts	20 sts
Needle 4:	20 sts	20 sts
Instep (Needles 1 and 2):	28 sts	24 sts
Heel (Needles 3 and 4):	40 sts	40 sts
WORKING THE GUSSET DECREASES		
Round 1 Needles 1 and 2 (instep): Work *Double* or *Single Rib Pattern* as established to end of each needle. Needle 3: K1, ssk, K to end of needle. Needle 4: Knit to last 3 sts, K2tog, K1.		
You now have	66 sts	62 sts
Round 2 Needles 1 and 2: Work Rib Pattern to end of each needle. Needles 3 and 4: Knit to end of each needle.		
Round 3 Needles 1 and 2: Work Rib Pattern to end of each needle. Needle 3: K1, ssk, K to end of needle. Needle 4: Knit to last 3 sts, K2tog, K1.		
You now have	64 sts	60 sts

	DK WT (SINGLE RIB)	WORSTED WT (DOUBLE RIB)
Repeat Rounds 2 and 3 until you have a total of	56 sts	48 sts
WORKING THE SOCK FOOT		
Note: You may adjust the foot length by working more or fewer rounds, as desired. Toe decrease is rounded and adds approximately 1½" (4cm) to sock length.		
Making no further decreases, work Rib Pattern as established over instep stitches and knit all sole stitches, until measurement from back of heel is	8¼" (20cm)	8½" (21cm)
SHAPING THE TOE		
Round 1 Needle 1: K1 ssk, K to end of needle. Needle 2: Knit to last 3 sts, K2tog, K1. Needle 3: K1, ssk, K to end of needle. Needle 4: Knit to last 3 sts, K2tog, K1. You now have	52 sts	44 sts
Round 2: Knit all stitches.		
Continue working Rounds 1 and 2 until you have	32 sts	28 sts
Repeat Round 1	4 times	4 times
You now have 3 stitches on each needle, for a total of	12 sts	12 sts
CLOSING THE TOE AND FINISHING THE SOCK		
In preparation for closing the toe, knit the 3 stitches from Needle 2 onto Needle 1. Slip 3 stitches from Needle 4 onto Needle 3. Break yarn, leaving a 10" (25cm) tail for closing the toe.		
Graft front and back stitches together using Kitchener stitch. (For instructions, see pages 29–30.) Weave in any loose ends. To block, lightly mist or steam sock and pat into shape.		

Shadow Box

A subtly textured stitch pattern is showcased between rolled top and rounded toe on these intriguing socks. A square shadow heel adds to the interest. This four-row repeat pattern is easy to learn, and the sock can be knit in either worsted or bulky weight. For a soft, luxurious sock, combine two yarns in the bulky version.

Size	Woman's medium–large
Yarn	**Bulky-Weight Version** Cascade Yarns Lana D'Oro, 50% Superfine Alpaca/50% Wool, worsted weight, 1.75 oz (50g)/110 yd (101m) skeins 3 skeins Granny Smith (#248) GGH Soft Kid, 70% Superkid Mohair/25% Polyamid/5% Wool, 0.88 oz (25g)/150 yd (137m) skeins 2 skeins Light Green (#054) Note: Hold one strand of each yarn throughout. For a Man's medium, use a larger needle to get a gauge of 16 stitches = 4" (10cm).
	Worsted-Weight Version (not shown) Cascade 220, 100% wool, 3.5 oz (100g)/220 yd (202m) skeins 2 skeins
Needles	**Bulky-Weight Version:** One 5-needle set US #5 (3.75mm) double-point needles, *or size you need to obtain correct gauge* **Worsted-Weight Version:** One 5-needle set US #3 (3.25mm) double-point needles, *or size you need to obtain correct gauge*
Gauge	**Bulky-Weight Version:** 18 stitches = 4" (10cm) in stockinette stitch **Worsted-Weight Version:** 24 stitches = 4" (10cm) in stockinette stitch
Other supplies	Tape measure, yarn needle, needle and stitch gauge
Abbreviations	**K** = knit; **K2tog** = knit 2 stitches together; **P** = purl; **P2tog** = purl 2 stitches together; **ssk** = slip, slip, knit the 2 slipped stitches together; **st(s)** = stitch(es); **wyb** = with yarn in back

GETTING STARTED	BULKY WT	WORSTED WT
Note: *Bulky Weight:* Hold one strand of each yarn together throughout. *Worsted Weight:* Use a single strand of yarn throughout.		
Setup: Loosely cast on	42 sts	48 sts
Divide onto 4 needles, as follows:		
Needle 1 (instep):	12 sts	12 sts
Needle 2 (instep):	8 sts	14 sts
Needle 3 (heel):	10 sts	10 sts
Needle 4 (heel):	12 sts	12 sts
Join into a round, being careful not to twist stitches. (For instructions, see Joining: Trading Places and Getting Ready to Work, page 16.)		
MAKING THE ROLLOVER SOCK TOP		
Option: If you don't want to make the rollover top, work 20 rounds K1, P1 ribbing, or to desired length.		
Rounds 1–10: Knit to end of each round (stockinette stitch).		
Rounds 11–20: K1, P1 to end of each round (ribbing).		
WORKING THE SOCK LEG		
Note: The beginning and end of each round will be on the right side of the foot as worn. You will be setting up the Shadow Box Pattern in the 4 rounds in this section. Instep for *Bulky Weight* has 3 pattern repeats plus P2. Instep for *Worsted Weight* has 4 pattern repeats plus P2.		
Bulky Weight only: **Round 1:** Knit to end of each needle.		
Round 2 Needle 1: *P2, K4; repeat from * to end of needle. Needle 2: P2, K4, P2. Needle 3: K4, P2, K4. Needle 4: *P2, K4; repeat from * to end of needle.		
Round 3: Knit to end of each needle.		

	BULKY WT	WORSTED WT
Round 4 Needle 1: *K3, P2, K1; repeat from * to end of needle. Needle 2: K3, P2, K3. Needle 3: K1, P2, K4, P2, K1. Needle 4: *K3, P2, K1; repeat from * to end of needle.		
Repeat Rounds 1–4 until piece measures 6½" (16.5cm), or desired length from cast-on edge, ending with Round 4.		
Worsted Weight only: **Round 1:** Knit to end of each needle.		
Round 2 Needle 1: *P2, K4; repeat from * to end of needle. Needle 2: *P2, K4; repeat from * to last 2 stitches, P2. Needle 3: K4, P2, K4. Needle 4: *P2, K4; repeat from * to end of needle.		
Round 3: Knit to end of each needle.		
Round 4 Needle 1: *K3, P2, K1; repeat from * to end of needle. Needle 2: *K3, P2, K1; repeat from * to last 2 stitches, K2. Needle 3: K1, P2, K4, P2, K1. Needle 4: *K3, P2, K1; repeat from * to end of needle.		
Repeat Rounds 1–4 until piece measures 6½" (16.5cm), or desired length from cast-on edge, ending with Round 3.		
MAKING THE HEEL FLAP		
Note: Let the instep stitches wait on Needles 1 and 2 while you knit the heel flap. Number of instep stitches:	20 sts	26 sts
Setup: Place the Needle 3 and 4 stitches on one needle. You will be working the heel flap back and forth using 2 needles. For the heel flap, you will have	22 sts	22 sts
Turn around last needle used (Needle 4) to begin to work back across on wrong side. This square heel has a 3-stitch garter stitch edging along both sides of the heel flap.		

	BULKY WT	WORSTED WT
Row 1: K3, P16, K3.		
Row 2: K3, *slip 1 wyb, K1; repeat from * to last 3 sts, K3.		
Row 3: Repeat Row 1.		
Row 4: K3, *K1, slip 1 wyb; repeat from * to last 3 sts, K3.		
Next Rows: Repeat Rows 1–4	3 more times	5 more times
Next Rows: Repeat Rows 1 and 2. The heel will measure approximately 2½" (6cm) and you will have just completed a right-side row.		
TURNING THE HEEL		
Beginning on wrong side, turn heel as follows:		
Row 1 (ws): P14 sts, P2tog, turn, leaving 6 sts unworked.		
Row 2 (rs): K7, ssk, turn, leaving 6 sts unworked.		
Row 3: P7, P2tog, turn, leaving 5 sts.		
Row 4: K7, ssk, turn, leaving 5 sts.		
Row 5: P7, P2tog, turn, leaving 4 sts.		
Row 6: K7, ssk, turn, leaving 4 sts.		
Row 7: P7, P2tog, turn, leaving 3 sts.		
Row 8: K7, ssk, turn, leaving 3 sts.		
Row 9: P7, P2tog, turn, leaving 2 sts.		
Row 10: K7, ssk, turn, leaving 2 sts.		
Row 11: P7, P2tog, turn, leaving 1 st.		
Row 12: K7, ssk, turn, leaving 1 st.		
Row 13: P7, P2tog, turn, leaving 0 sts.		
Row 14: K7, ssk, turn, leaving 0 sts.		
Heel turning complete. You now have	8 sts	8 sts

PICKING UP STITCHES FOR HEEL GUSSET	BULKY WT	WORSTED WT
Note: For techniques, see Secrets for Tight, Smooth Gussets, pages 26–29.		
Setup		
Using needle with remaining heel stitches, pick up and knit ___ along the right side of the heel flap.	11 sts	14 sts
On this needle you now have	19 sts	22 sts
Work Round 4 of the Shadow Box Pattern, set up under Working the Sock Leg, across the instep stitches on Needles 1 and 2. For the instep, you have	20 sts	26 sts
With empty needle (this now becomes Needle 3), pick up and knit ___ along left side of heel flap.	11 sts	14 sts
Onto same Needle 3, knit 4 stitches from remaining heel stitches. On Needle 3 you now have	15 sts	18 sts
Needle 4: Finish round by knitting remaining	15 sts	18 sts
You now have		
Needle 1:	12 sts	12 sts
Needle 2:	8 sts	14 sts
Needle 3:	15 sts	18 sts
Needle 4:	15 sts	18 sts
Total on all 4 needles:	50 sts	62 sts

WORKING GUSSET DECREASES

Round 1

Needles 1 and 2: Knit to end of each needle.

Needle 3: K1, ssk, K to end of needle.

Needle 4: Knit to last 3 sts, K2tog, K1.

Round 2

Needles 1 and 2: Work Shadow Box Pattern Round 2, as established in Working the Sock Leg.

Needles 3 and 4: Knit to end of each needle.

Round 3

Needles 1 and 2: Knit to end of each needle.

Needle 3: K1, ssk, K to end of needle.

Needle 4: Knit to last 3 sts, K2tog, K1.

	BULKY WT	WORSTED WT
Round 4 Needles 1 and 2: Work Shadow Box Pattern Round 4, as established in Working the Sock Leg. Needles 3 and 4: Knit to end of each needle.		
Next Rounds: Repeat Rounds 1–4 until you have	42 sts	48 sts
WORKING THE SOCK FOOT		
Continue working the four pattern rounds as established in Working Gusset Decreases, *but do not make any further decreases.* Work until piece measure 2" (5cm) less than desired sock length. Sock length measured from back of the heel is approximately 8" (20cm).		
SHAPING THE ROUND TOE		
Worsted Weight only: **Round 1:** Knit to end of round.		
Round 2: *K6, K2tog; repeat from * to end of round. You now have		42 sts
Rounds 3–4: Knit to end of each round.		
Both Weights: Continue worsted weight and begin bulky weight toe shaping.		
Rounds 5–6: Knit to end of each round.		
Round 7: *K5, K2tog; repeat from * to end of round. You now have	36 sts	36 sts
Rounds 8–9: Knit to end of each round.		
Round 10: *K4, K2tog; repeat from * to end of round. You now have	30 sts	30 sts
Rounds 11–12: Knit to end of each round.		
Round 13: *K3, K2tog; repeat from * to end of round. You now have	24 sts	24 sts
Rounds 14–15: Knit to end of each round.		

	BULKY WT	WORSTED WT
Round 16: *K2, K2tog; repeat from * to end of round. You now have	18 sts	18 sts
Round 17: Knit all stitches.		
Round 18: *K1, K2tog; repeat from * to end of round. You now have	12 sts	12 sts
Round 19: K2tog 6 times to end of round. You now have	6 sts	6 sts
CLOSING THE TOE AND FINISHING THE SOCK		
Break off yarn, leaving a 10" (25cm) tail. Using a yarn needle, tie off by running thread through the remaining 6 stitches.		
Weave in toe and any other loose ends.		

Resources

Blue Sky Alpacas
888-460-8862
www.blueskyalpacas.com
www.spudandchloe.com
Spud & Chloë Fine

Brown Sheep Company
800-826-9136
www.brownsheep.com
Wildfoote Luxury Sock

Cascade Yarns
www.cascadeyarns.com
Cascade 220, Cascade 220 Quatro, Lana D'Oro

Crystal Palace Yarns
www.straw.com
Crystal Palace Panda Silk

Dalegarn/Dale of Norway
www.dale.no/dalegarn
Dale Baby Ull, Falk

Fiber Trends for Naturally NZ Yarns
509-884-8631
www.fibertrends.com
Waikiwi Luxury Blend Sock Yarn

Lana Grossa
www.lanagrossa.com
Lana Grossa Meilenweit Cotton Fun, Meilenweit Cotton

Lorna's Hand-Dyed Yarns
773-935-3803
www.lornaslaces.net
Shepherd Sock Yarn

Louet North America
800-897-6444
www.louet.com
Gems Fingering Weight (Super Fine #1)

Misti Alpaca Yarns
888-776-9276
www.mistialpaca.com
Misti Alpaca Hand Paint Sock Yarn

Mountain Colors
406-961-1900
www.mountaincolors.com
Bearfoot

Westminster Fibers, Inc.
Yarn Division
800-445-9276
www.westminsterfibers.com
Regia 4-ply Sock Yarn, Regia Ringel Color, Regia 6-ply Design Line by Kaffe Fassett

Acknowledgments

More people than I can name contributed to this book. Thanks go first to my students, who raised wonderful questions and requested patterns to help them progress from basic to more challenging socks, and ultimately to patterns of their own.

Special thanks to: Evelyn Clark of Seattle, Washington, for encouraging me to write the book and supporting me through the whole process; Grace Jarvis of Corvallis, Oregon, for introducing me to sock knitting nearly 45 years ago; Sandy Blue of Seattle, Washington, for mentoring and encouraging me to design patterns and teach; Bev Galeskas of East Wenatchee, Washington, for sage pattern-writing advice; Nancy Bush and Lucy Neatby, and now many others, too, for wonderful sock books, inspirations, and new techniques. Other friends who provided help when it was needed: Mary Berghammer, Renee Coale, Sarah Hauschka, Jason Hanson, Judie Stanton and Annelie Wallbom. Again, special thanks and appreciation to Gwen Steege, creative and sensitive Storey Publishing acquisitions editor, who encouraged this book and contributed greatly to its development, and to technical editors Andrea Dodge and Kathy Brock.

Finally, heartfelt thanks go to my husband, Terry, for love, understanding, and support of all sorts through both editions of the book, to my children, Matthew (and Renee) Coale and Rebecca Skloot, for their love and long-time encouragement and to grandsons Nick (who can knit) and now Justin (who will).

For testing the patterns included in this book, thanks to: Rebecca Bienn, Kathleen Case, Mary Johnson, Ruth Ann Myers, and Carla Sawyer. Special thanks to Judie Stanton for knitting the socks "Best Foot Forward" and "Winter Garden" (shown on the cover) for this revised edition.

For providing yarn, thanks to:

Spud & Chloë Yarns (Blue Sky Alpacas), Cedar, Minnesota
Brown Sheep Company, Mitchell, Nebraska
Cascade Yarn Company, Tukwila, Washington
Crystal Palace Yarns, Richmond, California
Dale of Norway, Shelburne, Vermont
Fiber Trends (Naturally New Zealand Yarns), East Wenatchee, Washington
Lorna's Laces, Chicago, Illinois
Louet North America, Ogdensburg, New York
Misti Alpaca Yarns, Glen Ellyn, Illinois
Mountain Colors, Corvallis, Montana

Index

Page numbers in *italics* indicate photographs or illustrations. Page numbers in **bold** indicate charts.

Abbreviations

cc	contrasting color
K	knit
K2tog	knit 2 stitches together
mc	main color
P	purl
P2tog	purl 2 stitches together
psso	pass slipped stitch over
rs	right side
rnd(s)	round(s)
s2kp	slip 2 sts knitwise, K1, pass 2 slipped sts over knit stitch
ssk	slip, slip, knit the 2 slipped stitches together
st(s)	stitch(es)
St st	stockinette stitch
TW	twist right (K2tog leaving both sts on left needle, K again into front of first st on left needle and slip both sts off needle)
ws	wrong side
wyb	with yarn in back
wyf	with yarn in front
YO	yarn over

Other Storey Titles You Will Enjoy

2-at-a-Time Socks, by Melissa Morgan-Oakes.
An easy-to-learn new technique to banish Second Sock Syndrome forever!
144 pages. Hardcover with concealed wire-o. ISBN 978-1-58017-691-0.

101 Designer One-Skein Wonders,
edited by Judith Durant.
Patterns for every lonely skein in your stash, by knitwear designers from across the country.
256 pages. Paper. ISBN 978-1-58017-688-0.

The Knitting Answer Book, by Margaret Radcliffe.
Answers for every knitting quandry — an indispensable addition to every knitter's project bag.
400 pages. Flexibind with cloth spine. ISBN 978-1-58017-599-9.

Luxury Yarn One-Skein Wonders,
edited by Judith Durant.
The one-skein concept meets luxury fibers, including alpaca, silk, cashmere, and bamboo — fun, fast, and decadent!
272 pages. Paper. ISBN 978-1-60342-079-2.

Toe-Up 2-at-a-Time Socks, by Melissa Morgan-Oakes.
The practicality of toe-up knitting combined with the convenience of the 2-at-a-time technique!
176 pages. Hardcover with concealed wire-o. ISBN 978-1-60342-533-9.